BUILDING THE EXECUTIVE FUNCTION SKILLS
YOUR CHILD NEEDS IN THE AGE OF ATTENTION

YOUR KID'S GONNA BE OKAY

A GUIDE TO RAISING COMPETENT AND CONFIDENT KIDS

MICHAEL DELMAN, M. Ed

Your Kid's Gonna Be Okay: Building the Executive Function Skills Your Child Needs in the Age of Attention

For information about this title or to order other books and/or electronic media, contact the publisher:
Beyond BookSmart Inc.
460 Hillside Avenue
Needham, MA 02494
https://www.beyondbooksmart.com/
booksales@beyondbooksmart.com
Twitter: @BeyondBookSmart
Facebook: https://www.facebook.com/beyondbooksmart/

ISBN: 978-1-7320349-0-7

Printed in the United States of America

Cover design: Whitney Scharer
Interior design: 1106 Design

With gratitude for my mother, Judith Ann Brenner Delman, who provided wisdom, joy, and kindness to all who knew her, and for my father, Alan Delman, who has modeled integrity and a commitment to excellence. As far as I can tell, your kids turned out okay.

In loving memory of my aunt, Midge Lipkin, who led by example and brought enthusiasm to everything she did, and without whom, Beyond BookSmart, and therefore this book, would not have been possible.

And to the little boy on the train who I heard saying nicely to his mom, "Every day I dare you to listen to me. And to be nice to me!" You interrupted my work a bunch, kid, but you're spot on.

Table of Contents

Introduction

It seems like it was just a few years ago that we were living in the Information Age. Going to a top college meant having access to the best professors, who would share the most current knowledge with those privileged enough to attend. That emphasis on knowledge seems quaint now. It is a different world—one where being a walking encyclopedia does not guarantee success. Information is easy to attain; dealing with all that information is the new challenge. We are no longer in the Information Age, where knowledge reigns supreme. We are now in the Age of Attention, and, as a society, we are struggling to make the best use of the most precious commodities we have: our time and our attention.[1]

To manage the infinity of well-designed grabs for our time, focus, and money, we and, even more so, our children, need to master a different set of abilities known as Executive Function skills in the Age

---

[1] As Harvard professor Bob Kegan states, "If contemporary culture were a school, with all the tasks and expectations meted out by modern life as its curriculum, would anyone graduate?" Bear in mind that he wrote this about *adult* development! For more, see his book *In Over Our Heads: Meeting the Mental Demands of Modern Life.*

of Attention.[2] In a nutshell, Executive Function skills are generally regulated in a part of the brain known as the prefrontal cortex (PFC)[3] and help people set and achieve goals. More specifically, Executive Function skills include some of our most foundational abilities, such as being able to manage our impulses and emotions and being able to start tasks and stay focused on them. They also include more complex skills, such as being able to prioritize, plan, organize, problem-solve, and make adjustments when we're off base. As you can imagine, having problems with any one of these skills poses a challenge; if we see that our children have significant deficits in several of these skills, we naturally worry if they're going to be okay.

In this book, I will share with you the tools and strategies I have learned and/or developed over the past twenty-five years as a parent, teacher, school principal, and founder of the nation's largest Executive Function coaching company. I will also share a few of the many mistakes I made as a child, some just misguided, and others a bit more mischievous. The lessons I've learned were the result, not only of academic study, but of personal failures, journals full of reflection, and the ongoing decision to use myself as an experiment to see how much I could grow and improve.

My goal is to help you understand how children learn and grow, to add tools to your parenting repertoire, and to show you the skills you need to offer support in a way that your child will appreciate rather than resent. As a result, your child will become more capable and more confident both in school and beyond.[4]

---

[2] While the term "Executive Function" does not require capitalization, it tends to help those new to the term to see it as a title, so I will be using the convention of capitals for it throughout the book.

[3] Tap your forehead, but not too hard. That's where the PFC is located.

[4] If your child is at an age or has a temperament that makes them not receptive to your direct help, you can share some of the ideas found here with someone who may be in a position to exert greater influence in your child's life, such as a teacher or a favorite aunt or uncle.

Since academics are my own first love, they get the lion's share of examples in this book. As I've spent more than twenty-five years teaching, hiring and supervising educators, developing curriculum, and advising schools, academics are what I know best. In addition, school *is* where most kids spend a great deal of their time and energy: seven or more hours a day, 180+ days a year, for at least twelve years, not counting pre-school, kindergarten, college, and graduate school. Add in everybody's favorite activity—homework—and we are looking at the central part of a young person's life.

Moreover, school matters. Whether or not we remember and use the Pythagorean theorem every day, or discuss the ins and outs of ancient civilizations with our friends, we all need the broader Executive Function skills that school demands. To succeed in school, children need to learn how to control their impulses and treat others with respect, how to stay focused, how to break down directions, how to be aware of what they know and don't know and then seek help when they're stuck, how to stay organized and manage their time, and a host of other relevant skills that this book will explore. School matters because it's a training ground for life. School matters because it is a place where Executive Function skills, whether they are taught or not, are always expected.

The skills of managing frustrations, being persistent, and the rest of the Executive Function suite of tools apply anywhere we go. One parent, for example, recruited me to work with her son John, a junior in high school, on a number of issues. The goal was not only to do his very best on homework each night, but also to become a better writer and clean his room. He had no diagnosed learning disabilities, but he, like virtually all kids his age, still had Executive Function challenges, including starting "boring" tasks on time and staying organized. His mom was understandably concerned, since he was stalling out in several places. While she recognized that he had a lot going for him—he was kind, articulate, a standout in club soccer, and a leader in an extracurricular program—the improvements she felt he needed to make left her worried that he wouldn't be very successful when he went off to college and had to run his own life in just a couple of years.

In talking to John, I could see that he understood his mother's concerns, but he was only interested in improving his writing; he had no desire to perfect his homework or keep his room neat. I accepted these initial limits and focused on the writing, and after a few weeks, his mother did, too. After all, homework was getting done—albeit not to refrigerator-level quality—and nobody had been injured yet in his messy room, so we put those concerns on hold. Then, on a Sunday morning, I received an odd phone call, which was especially odd since he normally didn't call but texted me for our check-ins.

"Can you come over today, actually, like, now, if you could, and help me clean my room?" he asked. There was a degree of panic in his voice, which I ignored.

"Wow! You saw the light," I said. "What happened?"

"The soccer scouts are coming," he said, "and I'm supposed to be watched today. I can't find my jersey, and the coach said that in no circumstances would he play anyone who does not have their uniform. I didn't think it would be a problem to find it, but I can't. The game is at three."

"So, you don't want to clean your room. You just want to find your jersey, right?"

"Basically, yes."

I rushed over. We used a few sorting techniques to avoid redundant searches and within thirty minutes . . . he remembered where he had put it. While he didn't want to clean his room for the noble purpose of being neat and organized, he had discovered that, at times, knowing where everything was had real benefits. He admitted that his mother was right and that he wanted to do a better job on both the room and on his homework—maybe not at the level she wanted, but better than he had previously. He saw the benefit of being on top of things.

We spoke five years later, and I asked him how, as a young adult, he was doing with organization. He told me that for anything that really mattered, he had a dedicated space. He then added, "I've found that taking more responsibility for my life, such as doing my own laundry, has helped me since I have no one to blame but myself. I put the things down, so I'm more likely to know where they are." He just discovered over time that the adults were right. He has a full plate now: tutoring part-time, working as a business consultant, and applying to business school. I had always seen his potential; now, with course corrections he learned from Executive Function supports at home and through our work, with normal brain development, and with some real-world experience, he is comfortably making the transition to young adulthood. The kid's gonna be okay. So many kids are like this young man: They have strengths, but something is in their way.

This book untangles several of the most important obstacles to children's growth, confidence, and success, and offers solutions for helping them. Whether your children are typical learners or have specific learning challenges, such as ADHD or dyslexia, the skills discussed in this book will help you help them. The book begins in chapter 1 with motivation, the prerequisite to sustained effort. By focusing on the values implicit in having a motivated child, I aim to shift the conversation away from rewards and punishments and, instead, toward finding and emphasizing the intersection of your child's talents and passions. Chapter 2 uses an evidence-based model from psychology to explore how people change and how we can help facilitate that change in our children. Chapter 3 shows how we can help our children manage their anxiety, as we learn to manage our own worries about them. It addresses the question of how to achieve the optimal state of peak performance where our children are sufficiently motivated without being held back by fear of failure. Chapter 4 looks at attention, a skillset that includes task initiation (getting started), sustained attention (staying focused), and goal-directed persistence (finishing the job). This particular challenge is especially acute in the Age of Attention, when time-sucking activities are almost irresistible and so readily available. Chapter 5 explores the higher-level, more complex Executive Function skills such as prioritizing, planning, time management, and organization. Finally, chapter 6 examines the ability to reflect: how to learn and improve from experience.[5] This skill, as it develops, can serve as the master key to improving other areas.

Scratch beneath the surface of kids who seem lazy, oppositional, or bored, and you'll usually see young people with opinions, drive, and skills. Removing the impediments to their success and showing them how they can achieve their potential has been my life's work, and I hope that some of the successes, failures, and strategies I share in this book will help you to help them.

---

[5] While there are other Executive Function skills, such as processing speed (how quickly you can take in and make sense of information) and working memory (essentially, how effectively you can mentally juggle), this book does not attempt to cover every one. I have focused on the areas where I have found specific strategies that can garner the greatest gains.

An Overview of
Executive Functioning

"Executive Functioning" refers to the self-management skills that allow us to get things done. While we may get from point A to point B with our legs or wheels, it is our Executive Function skills that allow us to get there efficiently, to learn from the experience and to improve our approach. In the parlance of ADHD expert Russell Barkley, Executive Function is "the use of self-directed actions (self-regulation) so as to choose goals and to select, enact, and sustain actions across time toward those goals."[6] While the exact set of skills remains somewhat disputed among researchers, certain mental processes are imperative to managing ourselves and overcoming obstacles if we are to achieve these goals. These processes include the following:

- Controlling impulses and regulating our emotional state

- Starting tasks that we must do, even when we don't want to

---

[6] Barkley, *Executive Functions,* 104.

- Directing our attention effectively

- Setting priorities

- Planning tasks and managing time limits

- Organizing of materials and ideas

- Thinking flexibly

- Assessing our progress and changing tactics as needed

Executive Function skills follow a relatively consistent path of development. For example, toddlers can exert control over their impulses. However, they do not have the ability to determine priorities in a systematic way, a skill that does not typically begin until adolescence. Because of the variability among individuals, though, some people's Executive Function skills mature more quickly than others. As with physical development, these differences are readily observable by others. Unfortunately, unlike someone's physical growth, Executive Function weaknesses are poorly understood, so these kids often get labeled as "lazy" or "oppositional" instead of overtaxed, undersupported, and discouraged.

Until their challenges are understood, both adults and peers are likely to remain frustrated by kids with Executive Function difficulties. They may not think before speaking or posting on social media (impulse control), they may get upset easily since they often have difficulty managing their emotions (emotional regulation), they will find it difficult to focus for extended periods on challenging ideas and details (attention), and they're not usually aware of or committed to tackling their priorities. You can imagine the difficulty of running a household, managing a job, or being a strong student if these skills are significantly impaired.

Everyone struggles occasionally with being on top of things, or with one Executive Function skill or another. However, for some people, every day is a painful battle, and they feel like failures much of the time. For others, they are mystified by how much seems to go wrong, when their poor Executive Functioning is the cause of so many of the problems they create for themselves and those around them. It's not just losing the keys occasionally or being a few minutes late for meetings. For our kids, Executive Function deficits mean that they don't understand the directions in class. It means that they can't take notes without losing the thread of the presentation. It means that organizing themselves to write a paper, staying calm while studying for a test, or focusing on a book may be beyond their current abilities. Of equal concern, it may mean that people find them frustrating to be around since they don't follow through on commitments very well and often have trouble seeing the perspectives of others.

Fortunately, our Executive Function skills develop over time until our mid- to late-twenties.[7] In addition, because of what is known as neuroplasticity—the brain's ability to learn from experience and to change itself—Executive Functioning can continue to be protected and even improved in some ways throughout our lives.[8]

Can we, as parents, do specific things to support our children's development of Executive Functioning, to make those skills stronger sooner? The answer is an unequivocal "yes." To begin, we and our children need a "growth mindset," a belief that abilities are not

---

[7] "[The research of Dr. Jay Giedd of the National Institute of Mental Health] also showed that the brain areas responsible for more advanced cognitive processes—integrating information from the senses, abstract reasoning and judgment, and other "executive functions" (the prefrontal cortex) mature last—and not fully until the late twenties or early thirties." David Gleason, "Expecting Our Kids to Behave Like Adults."

[8] "In terms of cognitive interventions, actual gains in neural volume relative to a control group were demonstrated . . . when older adults were trained to juggle for 90 days." Park and Bischof, "The Aging Mind."

permanent, but something that can be developed. This mindset is not wishful thinking but real-world magic. Carol Dweck, the Stanford researcher who popularized the idea of growth mindsets, has demonstrated through brain imaging and interviews that those with the growth mindset respond to challenges by "engaging deeply, processing their errors, learning from them, and correcting them," while those who believe that ability cannot change "run from their errors."[9]

According to Adele Diamond and Kathleen Lee, citing a compilation of studies carried out through the National Institute of Health, myriad solutions exist that strengthen Executive Function skills beyond their regular course of development. From the right school environment to taking properly taught martial arts classes, from exercise to games, we can provide opportunities that capitalize on our children's strengths and others that help them improve where they struggle, being mindful that for every individual, the Executive Function profile is, indeed, a mix of strengths and challenges.[10]

Trying small experiments with our kids and improving the way we interact with them will help our children to develop these fundamental skills. Eventually, as they see the benefits of stronger Executive Functioning, they themselves will want to and be able to improve the skills on their own.

---

[9] Dweck, "The Power of Believing."
[10] Diamond and Lee, "Interventions Shown to Aid Executive Function."

Chapter 1

Before Skills: Cultivating Motivation

I went to the woods to live deliberately . . .
so that I would not come to find at the end
of my life that I had not lived at all.

—Henry David Thoreau, *Walden*

Introduction to Motivation: The *Sine Qua Non*

Who doesn't love a great Latin saying? *"Sine qua non"* translates, more or less, to "without which, there is nothing." Internal motivation is that one crucial ingredient without which real success is not possible.

In her seminal work *A Mind in the Making*, Ellen Galinksy shares the story of two groups of students taught study skills by Carol Dweck, the Stanford researcher mentioned earlier.[11] The children who received only six sessions but were also taught about the effect

---

[11] Galinsky, *A Mind in the Making*, 295–96.

of effort on success outperformed those who received eight sessions. In just several weeks, the professionals were able to teach the children how to think more effectively by having the right mindset. If they can achieve significant change in such a short time, consider how powerful the lessons are that we, as parents, teach our children day after day over the eighteen or so years that they live with us. This first chapter will review the key factors within our control that can help our children feel motivated on a regular basis.

Often, we end up spending so much energy in the day-to-day, trying to coax our kids to do their homework and clean their rooms, that it's easy to lose sight of their incredible possibilities. Even when we do know, it's tough to find the time and energy (and, for most of us, money) to help them pursue those interests and passions that will give their lives more joy and greater meaning. The irony is that when our children spend time on the activities at the intersection of their talents and their passions, the happiness and success they experience make us happier and give us more energy. We transcend that ugly feeling we have occasionally that raising our children is mostly a chore, an endless checklist of things we must do to avoid failure, both theirs and ours. What if our orientation was toward fulfillment and meaning and not just survival? Supporting our children in the pursuit of their passions also affirms that they matter, not just for our benefit as proud parents, but for their own satisfaction, for all that they as unique individuals bring to the world.

Something to Try . . . When You Want to Understand Your Child's Perspective

This exercise is an opportunity to check your assumptions about your child's interests. Begin by filling out a blank version of figure 1a.

What I Think My Child Loves	What I Think My Child Can't Stand	What I Want My Child to Love (including what he already loves)
Baseball	Reading	Reading
Minecraft	Family game night	Baseball
Ice cream		Time with the family

Figure 1a: Parent Assumptions

Now, talk to your child. For columns 1 and 2, ask your child what they love or hate, and check it off if you accurately predicted it. If you missed it, write it down with the phrase "didn't know." For column 3, ask your child, "What do you think that I want you to love doing?" Then, check it off if they guessed accurately, note it if they missed it, or add items they mention that you hadn't included. See the example in figure 1b.

What My Child Actually Loves	What My Child Actually Can't Stand	What My Child Thinks I Want Him to Love
Baseball – ✓	Reading – ✓	Reading – ✓
Minecraft – ✓	Family game night – no, he doesn't	Baseball – ✓
Ice cream – ✓	Math teacher – didn't know	Time with the family – he missed
Me! – didn't know he'd say that!		Math – his guess

Figure 1b: Checked Parent Assumptions

The results will provide some interesting information for you to consider. What kind of overlap is there between what you want for your child and what they love already? What about between what you wish for them and what they really loathe? How accurate are you and your child when it comes to knowing what the other wants? Now is not the time to try to change anything; you're just taking the temperature, gauging how close or far apart you are. Problem-solving comes later.

Parents: Wired for Survival, Not Satisfaction

Billions of our fellow human beings around the world struggle each day to survive, seeking food, clothing, and shelter, and avoiding the atrocities of war. The adults in these cases must focus on the critical matter of daily survival, not on long-term planning or reading a book like this that focuses on achieving success with sanity.

For those of us whose basic survival needs are taken care of, we have the privilege of being able to focus our energies on being successful and finding purpose in our lives. Although sometimes snarkily called "first-world problems," this progression from survival to self-actualization—articulated by Dr. Abraham Maslow as a hierarchy of needs—naturally unfolds for people as more basic needs are met.[12] It begins with basic biological necessities and progresses to self-actualization. See figure 2.

One of our greatest challenges as parents is that we are biologically wired to feel that our job is to help our children survive, even in cases when we intellectually recognize that they will survive and that we could, instead, focus on helping them thrive. Even when we have enough to eat and a decent place to live, even when our kids are no longer three years old and in danger of running into the street, we worry a lot. Even when our kids are relatively healthy and successful, we are wired to worry. Our words may be, "Getting

---

[12] "Maslow's Hierarchy of Needs."

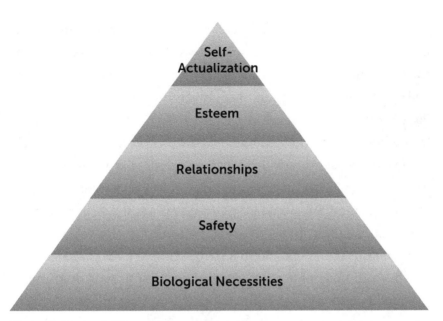

Figure 2: Maslow's Hierarchy

a C– is not acceptable in this house," but our unspoken worry may be that our kid will end up in some sort of danger, or will perhaps fail to become independent. Our biological imperative to protect our children is always operating at some level, even when it is neither necessary nor helpful.

As a result, we often end up playing defense and trying to prevent problems and, in the process, actually diminishing our children's opportunities. From a neurological point of view, the amygdala is largely to blame. The amygdala, a walnut-sized part of the brain responsible for intense emotions, is programmed to notice any potential threats and to respond with fear or anger, a fight-or-flight reaction.[13] Having a fear-based approach to parenting our children, while natural and understandable, interferes with our ability to help them become successful, confident, self-directed individuals

---

[13] There is a third response, "play dead," which appears as withdrawal.

who forge new and interesting paths for themselves. This limitation is especially negative in the modern world where the fast pace of change demands that they learn to think independently and quickly.

In the Age of Attention, our children need strong Executive Function skills and a sense of purpose if they are to succeed. Given the demands they will face, our job today is to help our children not just to survive, but to tap into their deepest interests and to find what value they can bring to the world by capitalizing on their strengths and managing their weaknesses. In doing so, in having that high level of motivation, they will bring their full capacities to whatever they attempt to do. Having that drive and purpose is a huge part of what will make them resilient and successful. As shown in the introduction, it may start with a soccer jersey, but that one teachable moment can open the door to becoming more responsible and better with Executive Functioning more generally.

All this may sound daunting, especially if what you see in your child today doesn't fit the image of what you deem necessary for success in the future. It's worth reiterating that people naturally develop their Executive Function skills until about age thirty, so the dramatic transformations I have seen so many times make sense from a developmental perspective. With a bit of patience and some well-placed support, the odds are that your kid is gonna be okay. We all know that caterpillars can turn into butterflies and acorns into oak trees.[14] Sometimes, though, because of the stress of parenting, we forget that it doesn't help to constantly worry about our children, just as we wouldn't worry every single day about saplings we had planted. We wouldn't ask ourselves, "Hmm, how come they didn't improve at all since yesterday?" Those trees take time to grow, and

---

[14] For an incredibly encouraging and insightful story that is worth reading, see Trina Paulus's *Hope for the Flowers*.

simply need to be given the right kind of nourishment to reach their potential. For our children, our patience, kindness, and encouragement will pay better dividends than constantly wringing our hands and telling them how anxious we are about them.

Something to Try . . . When You Worry About Your Child's Future

Find a quiet place and a time when you will not be disturbed, because this exercise may prove to be a bit uncomfortable and disturbing enough itself. Jot down your image of your child in the future if things go badly, if your child does not figure out how to get dressed independently each morning, if your child does not get homework done on time and with a reasonable degree of quality, if things continue in the same way that they have, with the same problems, only magnified as the demands of adulthood catch up with them. (If things are going great, but you're anxious anyway, then imagine if they started to unravel because of something that tends to make you anxious.) What does it look like? What would a video camera show? Where would your child be living? What would your child be doing each day? How would you be feeling? We're playing out the worst-case scenario here.

Now, for a contrast, try writing down what it would look like if your child were getting the basics done and able to support him- or herself. What are they doing with their lives? Who are they with? How are you feeling?

Finally, what would it look like if your child was wildly successful and happy as an adult? What might they be doing for work? Who would your child be spending time with? How are you feeling here? See figure 3 for an example.

	DISASTER SCENARIO	LIKELY SCENARIO	IDEAL SCENARIO
MY CHILD	Dropped out of college after one year, depressed, living at home, alternates between blaming us for being bad parents and herself for being a failure.	College was great, working at a stepping-stone job, needs some cash at times but appreciates it, thinks we're okay.	College graduate who got dream job after a few years, self-sufficient, thanks us for the support and the tough love.
ME	We share her opinion—we failed, and she failed, and we're frustrated most of the time, especially since she is living in our space.	We enjoy her and feel confident that she'll be in good shape by the time she's thirty.	We miss her but are happy she doesn't need us too much now. We're overjoyed for her.

Figure 3: Visions of the Future

Envisioning these contrasting futures opens doors. If you can't see the third vision, it may be difficult for your child to see it. If you can only see problems in the future, that will influence your child's belief about the future. While almost any future is possible, the ones we spend time focused on give us energy and sometimes insight to move in that direction.

Unintended Consequences: Expectations as the Anti-Motivator

Sometimes, in trying to motivate our children to do their best, we inadvertently burden them with unrealistic expectations that have the opposite effect of what we intended. Particularly with school as a central point of conflict, we sometimes convey messages either through our words or actions that are counterproductive. The following expectations, while fairly common, can have serious side effects, yielding results we do not want.

Expectation #1: My kid should get all A's and/or be the best student in the class

This expectation clearly can't be true for everyone. Only one student can be the best in any class, and most schools aren't designed to allow *everyone* to achieve at the highest level, since A's mean outstanding, and some students have to be average and others below average for these kinds of grades to mean what they were designed to represent. In addition, parents do not typically have sufficient information about the competition, the other students, to know what rank is reasonable for their children. Finally, it is worth considering that all A's may actually be too easy for some students. For some children, there are times when the subject material is not sufficiently challenging for them. An externally based goal is not the best place to begin.

Expectation #2: My child should try their hardest in school

We want our children to work hard in school, but why? If the aim is *not* for them to be the best, what makes us feel that our children should try their very best in school? How much of this conviction comes from our fear of being judged because our kids are not working to their potential? Will people think that perhaps we don't care enough about our children, or that we are ineffective parents? We all recognize that those societal voices come to us from our family members, our schools, and the various media we consume; but in the end, we have to take responsibility for listening to them, since we have internalized these societal norms. What if those voices were not only mistaken, however, but damaging?

This book unabashedly promotes a different view: that our kids will be happier and more successful if they try their hardest *selectively*. If an assignment is worth more points, it merits greater effort than a low-point assignment. If it's not graded or worth little, it's not worth as much time unless your child is interested in the material. If the assignment gets your child pumped up, then it is, by definition, worth the time. Human beings have a unique capacity for learning, and if our children are already motivated, we generally just want to move out of the way and allow them to go further.

Expectation #3: I need to motivate my child

It's understandable to feel that we need to motivate our children. Our actions do affect our children's attitudes and effort, and we can feel that we are failures as parents if our kids aren't doing what is expected of them. However, our children are governed in many ways by their own mysterious interests. They are driven by their own motives, not just ours. Consequently, "How can I motivate my child?" may not be the question to ask. A question to consider, instead, is "How can I help my child find what moves them, what gets them motivated, and how can I set up those conditions so they find their own sense of purpose and drive?"[15]

Until they hit early adolescence sometime between the ages of ten and thirteen, most children love to please us. We leverage our relationship for a host of things: to hurry them along, to get them into the dentist's seat, to persuade them to be nice to their siblings, and so on. Then school comes along, and we have, dare we admit

---

[15] While this chapter emphasizes helping your child discover what personally motivates them, the next chapter discusses how to help your child tackle the mundane and frustrating things that they avoid.

it, competition. Other adults are now motivating our kids, and they have an arsenal of tools that we don't possess. They can use the power of the group setting to build norms and set expectations. They can assign scores and grades that add pressure. Plus, these educators are professionals and know all sorts of tricks that most parents don't, such as how to create games to make the material more interesting, or how to connect new lessons to previously learned material.

Still, our kids depend on us for so much, and we can motivate them in many ways—with our compliments and our hugs, and, when we need a little extra, with rewards and punishments. We try not to threaten and use bribes too much, but we also see how quickly we can shut down a protest and use those tools to get them to do what we want. Sometimes when we control their behavior, it is ostensibly for them—so that they will be successful, stay out of trouble, and reap other unnamed benefits. At other times, we admit that we are manipulating their behavior to make our lives easier—so that things get done around the house, so they will not embarrass us by standing out in any negative way, and so on. The underlying message in either case is that we expect our children to comply; if they do, they will be on our good side and will be treated better.

Unfortunately, that path goes places we might not choose if we could see to the end of it. When we control and manipulate our children with bribes and threats, rewards and punishments, they don't develop an internal compass. The children who spend too much of their energy "aiming to please," something often meant as a compliment, do not develop a strong sense of self and can't develop a deep sense of confidence. In addition, they lack a sustainable commitment to what they are doing, and the setbacks they are bound to encounter will expose their superficial commitment to doing well. In the long run, as these children mature into young adults, they often resent those adults whom they have been trying so hard to please and give up on those things that were pushed on them.

Of course, there are times when we must insist that they do or do not do certain things in order to protect their best interests. These kinds of things—health and safety issues, for example—do not lead to longer-term problems in the relationship, or in our children being sapped of their own internal motivation. While our children may be temporarily frustrated with us for saying "no" when we feel it is necessary for their well-being, most understand that in these matters, we are doing our job as parents and probably know best or, at the very least, we have their interests at heart. We also need to have them contribute in an age-appropriate way to the family. These expectations are not about us motivating them; they are about us as responsible adults protecting them as needed and teaching them what it means to be part of a family.

It is only when we try too hard to sell them on who they "should" be or what they "should" do that we hurt their motivation. It is only when we impose a moral judgment about the value of their choices that we diminish their personal responsibility and decision-making and stir up resentment. Learning to let go of these three expectations—our kids being the best or achieving perfect scores, our kids always trying their hardest, and we as parents being responsible for motivating our kids—allows a much deeper and more sustainable internal motivation to develop.

One thing to consider in making adjustments to our expectations is the expectations our own parents had of us when we were children, especially when we were the ages our children are now. Which of those were really helpful to you? How did your parents convey them to you? Which of those expectations were not helpful? Consider what it was about the expectations that made them unhelpful: Was it the way they were expressed to you (e.g. unsolicited, or said in anger), or was it the content of the expectations (e.g. too hard, too easy, irrelevant)? Which of these approaches would you like to avoid in raising your own child?

Being a Tiger Teacher: The Value of Personal Investment

One year, when I was teaching sixth grade, I tried an experiment in motivation. To remove the stress of grades and to have students focus on quality work, I told my writing students that they would all be getting A's on their next paper. Joyful pandemonium ensued for a moment or two; then, some of them realized that there had to be a catch. The deal, I told them, was that they would need to improve their papers, with my feedback, until they achieved an A-level paper. It didn't matter how many tries it took; I would work with them on it until they succeeded. Joy turned to confusion.

"What if we don't want to get the A and we're okay with a B?" one brave and honest lad ventured to ask.

I was prepared for this. "Not an option," I replied. "Everyone will keep going until they get there. I want you all to know that you are capable of getting an A if you push through and receive the proper support."

I explained that they could move on to other writing once they had met all the standards on the rubric. To my surprise, many of the students then reacted not with appreciation for a guaranteed A, but with fear and frustration at the requirement to produce work at what they believed was an impossible level. Because of my role as their teacher, I was able to carry the assignment through to the end, and, indeed, many of the students achieved at higher levels than they had previously. I was behaving as a Tiger Teacher, making sure that my students met the ambitious goal I had set for them.[16] In one way, I succeeded; a number of students came to realize that they had more potential than they had been able to imagine.

However, some of the students gave up in spite of my guarantee, leaving me in a strange position of punishing them with extra help they did not want. Without a degree of choice, even a "reward" can be a punishment. With force, there can be little expectation of enthusiasm. In retrospect, I would have had better results with this group of students if I had given them the chance to determine the grade they wanted—not necessarily an A, perhaps, and perhaps with a minimum of a B—and promised them that they could and would receive that grade if they put forth the necessary effort, an effort that I would commit to matching. That would have shown that I had a balanced interest both in their achieving at the highest level possible and in respecting their own interests as individuals who, ultimately, were permitted to make decisions for themselves.[17] That approach could have motivated *all* of the students to achieve at the highest level.

⠇☀⠇ Something to Try . . . When Setting Meaningful Goals with Your Child

Ask your child what their goal is for something that matters to them: a test or paper, a sports event, an art project. Offer to help them if

---

[16] See Amy Chua's funny, valuable, and, at times, heartbreaking book *Battle Hymn of the Tiger Mother* for an example of a mom openly discussing her decisions to push her kids as hard as possible. Would you keep dinner and water from your child and not allow her to use the bathroom until she had completed a task you felt she could accomplish in order to teach her to persevere?

[17] A significant book has been co-written by mindfulness guru Jon Kabat-Zinn and his wife, Myla, about the importance of respecting the "sovereignty" of our children. Kabat-Zinn and Kabat-Zinn, *Everyday Blessings*.

they would like, and respect their "no" if they would rather do it by themselves. After the grade comes back, let them tell you how they felt about their performance compared to their goal. This will allow your child to be the one to drive the process and to develop a sense of what is good enough to bring about their satisfaction.

If your child is sufficiently motivated, use the SMART goals approach below.[18] SMART goals allow us to focus on something we care about for a specified amount of time and to know whether or not we have succeeded. Have your child name a goal that meets the following criteria:

S: Specific. Instead of a lofty intention, the goal is something that can be named and seen if it is accomplished, such as "improve my English grade this quarter." It is not something vague or generic, such as "be a better student."

M: Measurable. The goal is one that can be quantified, such as "getting a 90 percent or better for homework," and not "improve homework."

A: Assignable. The goal is clearly the responsibility of your child. "I will go in for extra help once a week" is better than "my teacher and I will have a strong relationship," which is only partly within the control of your child.

R: Realistic. The goal is one that is a bit of a stretch but still possible.

T: Time-relevant. The goal is one that has a starting point and a deadline. "I will get at least a B+ on my science labs this quarter" gives a clear period of time for reporting on and evaluating progress.

---

[18] The term "SMART goals" was coined by George Doran in 1981. Doran, "There's a S.M.A.R.T. Way to Write," 35–36.

Thoughtful Decision-Making: The Value of Informed Choice

A critical part of helping our children become motivated is to give them the power to make important choices while making sure that their choices are informed. When parents were considering sending their children to the charter school I founded, they frequently asked me whether they should allow their child to make the decision about which middle school they would attend. It was, to be sure, a big decision, one with three important years of schooling as the consequence.

While the maturity of the student was always a factor in the "decision about who makes the decision," it wasn't always possible to advise a family on whether their particular child was mature enough to make the final call, as so many variables were involved. The first critical step for them, then, was to gather information so that the process was good and the outcome had a better chance of being the right one for the child. In this case, the student and parent could attend an open house and a "shadow" day to attend classes. In doing so, the child would get a sense of what they would be saying "yes" or "no" to. Since this decision was about which school would best guide their child's intellectual development, moral compass, and social scene for the formative middle school years, the families felt it was worth the additional time to do the research and involve their child, so that, together, they could make an informed choice.

In a similar fashion, when our children are young, we open doors for them by exposing them to a wide range of opportunities, challenges, experiences, and perspectives. We may love piano, but they may like the saxophone, karate, golf, art, or any number of things we would not have anticipated until we saw the smiles on their faces. By being open to their ideas, we have better odds of finding that tremendous opportunity that might otherwise have lain dormant.

We don't need to require them to stick with something indefinitely, but we certainly want them to know enough to make good decisions.

Second, as our children get older, we need to give them increasing space. They naturally love to learn, and when they're enjoying some success, they want to become more independent and discover the full range of their capabilities. As most parents know, telling our children what to do is a relatively reliable way to get them to not want to do it. If our endorsement is too enthusiastic, we can stir our children's natural rebelliousness, which is especially sad when they themselves were already motivated. I remember how shocked I was when my younger daughter told me, "Dad, when you push me to practice something I already like doing, it makes me not want to do it." Apparently, we had let her read the parenting manual, and she now expected me to live up to it and give her some space.

Some kids find these passions early, and it is very clear to parent and child alike in those cases. Even if their talent isn't as robust as their passion, they are likely, with dedication and mentoring, to become quite good at their passion. I have found that, in the long run, those who have a great work ethic and who learn from their experience significantly outperform those who may have a great deal of natural talent but who are not as motivated, who undermine themselves through lack of self-discipline, or who lack strong Executive Function skills.

Finally, for those kids who do not find themselves motivated at a young age by a specific passion or a cluster of passions, there is nothing to worry about. Passion is not the only factor that drives success and happiness; it is just one of those magic elements that, when present, serves to magnify skills. For plenty of kids, the more generic motivation of wanting to be proud of their successes can keep them engaged until they do find a particular pursuit that truly speaks to them.

Something to Try . . . When Learning About Your Child's Interests

Ask your child what they love to do. When they tell you, instead of asking them why, which can provoke a defensive reaction, ask them what, as in: "What do you love about it?" Asking this question shows that you are genuinely interested in hearing more and that you won't be judging their response. If, for example, your child says they love video games, resist the urge to sigh or to be otherwise dismissive of their passion. (Sometimes we parents roll our eyes, too). Once you dig into the aspects of what draws them to an activity, you've got some valuable information about what fuels their interests and, better yet, a handle on how to link skills from what feels like a "useless" pastime to areas such as school or eventually a career. A kid who loves video games, for example, may enjoy them for the challenge of solving problems, for the pleasure of collaborating with friends on a similar mission, or for the thrill of competition. Imagine how useful those interests would be in the world outside of video games! In cultivating motivation in our kids, it's helpful to shift our emphasis to the skills behind the activities, and when the opportunity arises, make a connection to ways they can leverage those abilities in other contexts. A kid who's stressing about a group project at school may benefit from a reminder about the ways they gain consensus from their gaming buddies as a springboard to apply those skills elsewhere.

From Piece to Masterpiece: The Value of Personal Relevance

To achieve a high degree of success in anything, our kids will need a deep level of commitment to what they are doing. That commitment comes from personal relevance, which itself comes from some combination of natural talent and personal experience. I know many great educators, for example, who are inspired to be great, either because they have a learning disability themselves, or are close to someone with a learning challenge. In both cases, they feel a deep satisfaction in helping others to manage or to overcome those challenges. Whatever it is that our kids will pursue—whether it is the beauty of music, the thrill of doing battle in the sports arena, or seeing fascinating connections in the worlds of the sciences—the activity, topic, or issue needs to stir something in them if they are to go as far as they can.

Several great papers of my students exemplify the point. The first was a research paper for a history class, the topic of which was my personal favorite: "Choose your own topic, but cite the heck out of it." The student chose the international politics of baseball, and, well, he hit it out of the park. From how the Major Leagues recruit and take advantage of players from Latin America, to the burgeoning interest in Japan at that time, his documentation was phenomenal. Another student wrote his college essay about his brother returning home from college and coming out about identifying as male when he had been raised as a female. Few readers could have seen it coming based on the introduction, and the paper explored in depth the insights the applicant had about himself based on the courage of his brother. One student explored his high school's atrocious schedule that led to sleep deprivation among students, a problem whose ramifications include an elevated risk of depression, diminished intellectual functioning, and "drowsy driving," which can be as dangerous as drunk driving, depending on the level of deprivation.

In all of these cases, the writing was elevated from a piece to a masterpiece because the students felt inspired to write about what mattered to them. As a result, they went far beyond the expectations and received tremendous results, from getting high A's on the papers, to getting into top colleges with the help of these great essays.

Success, of course, led to more success, as these results inspired them to continue to focus their energies on additional opportunities to write about these topics and to pursue their interests in other venues. I have seen this sort of positive cycle over and over. A student learns some of the basic Executive Function skills to achieve basic success—how to start (task initiation) and stay focused (sustained attention) while being calm (emotional regulation)—and an adult that the child admires reinforces that they didn't simply get lucky. Instead, they put in effective effort, and if they do the same thing next time, they have a very good shot at getting similar results.

It takes courage for schools to allow students some freedom to pursue their passions, whether in choosing their reading books, writing topics, or subjects of study, and for us as parents to advocate for such opportunities. We also, of course, can encourage our kids to find what matters to them at home. It brings rewards twice over: Our kids are happy and successful because they have found what they love, and they will feel grateful—if not now, then when they get a bit older—that we value them for who they are, not just for doing well at what is expected of them.

Something to Try . . . When Your Child's Greatest Concerns Could Become Their True Passions

Ask your child to make a list with you about things they feel are wrong with the world. The "world" can be defined broadly to include their school, things at home, in their town, and so forth. This list opens the door to what they might want to do to improve the world, and having a cause is one of the great ways to have a sustained passion. Kids have a sense of justice and injustice and often wish they could do more about the things that bother them. They may even discover a career that allows them to rectify the situation. The student who was frustrated about sleep deprivation and getting to school on time could conduct scientific research or advocate for schools to change their start time, a trend that is gaining momentum across the country. Plenty of fascinating (and paid) jobs already exist in areas we may not personally know about, and if a job does not yet exist, there is an opportunity for your child to create it.[19] Start with the interest, and see how far it can go.

Success and Failure: The Value of Stretching Limits[20]

A mom at one of my presentations asked me what to do about her son, a junior in high school, whose school troubles began before his feet even hit the floor each day; he simply refused to get out of bed in the morning. She acknowledged that this attitude applied to nearly every aspect of his life. She felt that he had the capacity to do much more for himself, but she struggled to manage her own anxiety about the potential consequences if she allowed him to fail. For example, would he lose a credit in one of his classes if she didn't get him up? If so, would she have been negligent?

Micromanaging our children by solving their problems for them and ensuring that they never fail delays the development of their skills and diminishes their incentive to push themselves.[21] While our kids need us to be kind and encouraging in order to reach their potential, they also need to know as they get older that they will be okay without our regular intervention, a belief that will only develop

---

[19] A friend of mine is actually the Director of the Center for Sleep and Cognition through Harvard, so I know that that job is possible.

[20] See Kate Losse, "The Art of Failing Upward."

[21] See Wendy Mogel's books *The Blessing of a Skinned Knee* and *The Blessing of a B Minus: Using Jewish Teachings to Raise Self-Reliant Children.*

if they see proof that it's true. By trying to figure out most things on their own instead of going to us at the first sign of trouble, our children learn how to persevere and come to understand that an initial failure now can actually be a step toward doing better.

Unfortunately, the statistics about our young adult children do not show such resilience but, rather, an epidemic of students failing to make the transition from high school to college. The National Student Clearinghouse Research Center shows that more than 40 percent of college freshmen will take at least six years to graduate—if they ever do at all.[22] Dr. Laurence Steinberg has shown that a year or two of a four-year college program does not add any benefit to a student's earning potential, a costly investment to lose.[23]

For some students, the problem is that they are not interested in immediately continuing their education right after school. They would do better working as they explore the question more deeply as to why they want to go to college. Other students are motivated but have not yet developed the Executive Function skills necessary to transition successfully from the high level of structure and support they receive during high school to the tremendous freedom they will have in college. It is critical to teach and test those skills gradually, over time, and well ahead of that freshman year of college. Success is sweet, but failure is good food, and they need enough of that gritty nourishment while young to be tough enough for the challenges that lie ahead. If we prepare our children well, then they will become increasingly independent, achieve meaningful successes, and learn from the obstacles they have overcome.

---

[22] According to the National Student Clearinghouse Research Center, only 53 percent of students graduated college within six years, let alone four years—an expensive endeavor made even more expensive. Bidwell, "Most Students Don't Graduate."
[23] Steinberg, *Age of Opportunity.*

Something to Try . . . to Encourage Out-of-the-Box Thinking

At this time, who is it that challenges your child in a way that has a positive effect: you, a professional, or a friend of your child? Are they doing so methodically, as a well-trained professional would, or do they just happen to inspire your child? Having a mix of both the well-planned, deliberate pushes that a dedicated coach would provide and more personal situations where the interaction is less predictable is ideal; the former produces reliable growth while the latter develops flexibility.

Ask your child something like this: "If you could create your own school and stop going to normal classes, and instead focus on learning about anything at all that interests you, what would you study? Any answer is fine, as long as you would be willing to put in many hours every day of your own time toward becoming an expert." Your child might say "dogs" (my younger daughter's first answer for many years), or you might find that it's something more traditionally focused on in school, such as science. The important thing is to let your child know that since success requires considerable effort, you support them in pursuing their interests—and that doing so will take persistence.

Reflective Quitting: The Value of Prioritizing

In order to achieve at high levels, stay motivated, and maintain focus on those points of intersection between talent and passion, it is important to make choices not only about what one *will* do but also about what one will *not* do. Our kids can do almost anything, but they definitely cannot do everything. We know this is true for us given how busy we are, but it's at least as important to apply it to our children as well. Focusing on what matters allows our kids to be more successful at the few things that they choose, and also to be happier than if they try to do too much.

While it is good, initially, to have exposure to many opportunities, it's also okay and even beneficial for our kids to drop those activities that do not mean a great deal to them. Decisions, from the Latin to "cut away," are about removing what is not important so that important things get done. Some of those things we will eliminate may be of some value or considered worthwhile by others but are not as high priority as other choices, and, therefore, do not "make the cut." To begin with the obvious, we can consider the relative value of—and significantly limit—the indisputable time-wasters in our lives, such as most social media, games, and watching shows and videos.[24] We can set parameters for these time bandits using designated breaks and a timer, so that we don't "accidentally" let the next episode start.

In addition, we can teach our children how to quit when the going gets useless. While the word "quitting" usually has a negative association, it does not necessarily indicate a character defect. Quitting smoking takes discipline. Quitting a job that has no intrinsic satisfaction and no upward mobility can show courage. Quitting an abusive relationship means valuing oneself enough to leave something bad. We may push and at times require our children to do some things that we believe they must do in order to have opportunities later in life. For longer-term commitments, however, some things are undoubtedly a better fit for them than others.

The question, then, is not a negative one about whether it is okay to quit; it's a positive one about what deserves our children's attention and how much. Quitting dance, piano, or soccer may be

---

[24] Of course, shows of great social and educational value, such as *Stranger Things* or *Brooklyn Nine-Nine*, are worth whatever time one must invest to fully grasp them.

necessary to give your child the time to focus on something even more appealing to them. In the end, it's about return on investment. Which activities will make them happiest? Which will help them to mature? If you are considering impact on their college resume, then make it a conscious choice. It may be tricky to decide how much to weigh some of these competing values, but it's important to ask the questions. The answers will help in dealing with the reality that they cannot do everything. The very act of choosing to continue or to let go makes what they keep even more valuable.

Figure 4 is a schematic showing some of my older daughter's activities when she had too much to do at the age of thirteen. Given her busy schedule, we put each activity up against every other activity to see which she valued more. Then, we totaled the "wins" for each activity and took a close look at the winners and losers. With zero votes for cello lessons, we stopped that activity to give her time to focus on other activities that were higher priority for her, such as doing her homework well and preparing effectively for her bat mitzvah.

ACTIVITY	Homework	Dance	Bat Mitzvah	Cello	Piano
Homework (8)	X	H	H	H	H
Dance (2)	H	X	B	D	P
Bat Mitzvah (6)	H	B	X	B	B
Cello (0)	H	D	B	X	P
Piano (4)	H	P	B	P	X

Figure 4: Prioritizing Matrix

I had actually wanted her to continue with the cello. I think it's a cool instrument. I love the sounds it makes, and I think it builds character to master an instrument. However, by allowing her to make her own decisions over the years, we have seen her blossom in the things that she values the most. Cello is out, but piano is in and at a higher level. It's also more relevant to her interest in musical theater. Over time, she also shifted priorities to emphasize dance, and she has seen herself make great strides there as well.[25]

Given the overly stimulating world in which we live and the number of options we have to occupy our time, it is more important than ever to be deliberate in what we require our children to spend their time doing. Kids find their passions faster and are far more motivated if they are allowed to drop activities once they have given them a reasonable try.

☼ Something to Try . . . When Your Child Has More Activities Than Time

The matrix exercise in figure 4 generally takes about thirty minutes to complete and yields some wonderful insights if you come in with an open mind. Establish from the start that you are doing this together to gain information, but that you will be making the final call (if that is the case). During the exercise, resist the urge to influence your child's choices based on your own perspective. Let them discover their own preferences when faced with an either/or choice. That's the whole point of the exercise. Of course, it's a good idea to preface the activity with setting some expectations. If your child decides

---

[25] Really, she's made leaps and bounds here. Consider skipping the footnotes to avoid the worst jokes in the book.

homework is never a priority when comparing it to other activities, they don't get to ditch their homework entirely.

Another variation is for each of you to do the exercise separately, and then to compare notes with your child. Finally, these exercises also work best if you've tried them on yourself for your own activities first. The process of completing this exercise, in particular, tends to lead to some epiphanies about what is worth our time, and where we will want to let other things go.

I'd Rather Be Working: The Value of Finding Your Passion

It is a blessing to find the intersection of raw talent and total enthusiasm. That's the easy case, and it's pretty rare, as with our older daughter, Jenna, who, for as long as I can remember, has been singing—at home, in the grocery store, in the car, everywhere. To give her an outlet, we signed her up for a "Broadway Babies" troupe when she was four years old. Situated in a small church at the time, the director had the kids sing Disney songs in a group and gave each one of them a solo. Some of these solos were a bit tough on the ears, but the kids all had a great time.

When my daughter took the mic and started singing her first solo, I noticed that other parents stopped their conversations, and Sam, the director, had tears on her face. While I had always thought that Jenna was really good at singing, I didn't have anything to compare it to until then. That was a turning point for me in realizing that I needed to nurture her gift in any way I could, as this was her area of natural motivation. We also can see it when our child is really enthusiastic about something. If your child can't stop thinking about or talking about something, you've landed on something important. If she's staying up late taking notes or reading about it online, it's worth further exploration.

One of my former students is a terrific musician and hopes to make a living out of some aspect of music. He succeeded in getting into and graduating from the Berklee College of Music in Boston, and then getting hired at a top-notch recording studio in New York City. Although he earns a low wage, he is adding something important to his resume, gaining valuable experience, and building a network of connections. In all of this, he is continuing on his mission-driven approach. He is working insane hours, but he is happy in the present and working toward a future that excites him. Another former student of mine took time away from a prestigious college to work various jobs in the entertainment industry, network among talented professionals, and develop his own comedy routines and YouTube videos. Today's students have a plethora of opportunities to pursue their passions that may not necessarily involve a straight climb up the traditional ladder.

If you observe your child being completely swept up in building, creating, or practicing something—not just passively watching something or commenting on other people's work—then you may be so lucky as to have a child who has found a calling. Of course, you will still need to tell them to get some sleep, but you can feel good about the motivation they have. Does your child carry a journal for their thoughts or keep notes of great ideas in their phone? As parents, we can and must guide our kids a bit on the importance of maintaining healthy habits, but an occasional dose of overdoing it may demonstrate a true passion for something. As Oscar Wilde said, "Everything in moderation . . . including moderation."

Role Models: The Value of Authenticity

As is the case for anything we want to teach, one of the best methods for developing our children's motivation is to embody what we want our children to learn. We teach best if we ourselves have the motivation and the Executive Function skills we want our children to have. As Ralph Waldo Emerson said, "Don't say things. What you are stands over you."[26] We, too, need to pursue our passions, professionally if possible and in other ways if not. It's not just for our kids to witness. It's for their direct benefit. As the saying goes, "If Momma ain't happy, ain't nobody happy." If we pursue some of the things we love and show that we are constantly learning and fascinated by challenges, we are both modeling for our kids and keeping ourselves young. Spending energy on what we love gives us more energy for our kids.

We don't have to be tremendously wealthy or famous to serve as role models; we just need to have pursued something meaningful with our heart really in it. Even if it's about accomplishments from our past, our kids benefit from seeing that we were able to motivate ourselves. Whether it's talking to them about paying our way through college, serving in the Peace Corps, starting a small business—regardless of its financial success—or having pushed ourselves hard on the athletic field, we can show our kids that we understand at a personal level the joy of committing ourselves to something tough but worthwhile.

And so it's worth considering what you yourself love to do and then make time for it. What drives you? How do you manage to make time for it even when you are busy? Do you overdo it sometimes in this endeavor . . . but love it? How can you help your child to have

---

[26] Emerson, *Letters and Social Aims.*

more time for something in their life that they love and that requires real effort on their part?

> ## Something to Try . . . So You Can Lead by Example

Tell your children about your passions. Better still, show them enough that they get a little insight into what makes this activity or interest exciting to you. They may not follow in your footsteps, at least not now, but they will likely respect you for having interests outside of taking care of them. Showing them that you make time for what is important to you, for what you find fulfilling, encourages them to find that passion for themselves.

In addition, see if you can expose your kids to others who live their dreams, preferably in person but through biographies and auto-biographies as well. If they don't meet and gain insight into people who have truly pushed themselves, then they may not even believe it's possible. Show them that it's not just "special people" who have done this, but all sorts of people, often folks who have overcome the odds. Help them shift from being jealous of successful people, a reaction many of us might feel at first, to being inspired. You can certainly use examples of famous people, but neighbors and family members are also very helpful in showing that we can at least pursue, and perhaps even achieve, great things in our lives.

Breakdancing Through Life: The Value of Joy

When I was in college, a traffic cop gained some notoriety for directing cars by using breakdancing moves. People went out of their way to watch him do his thing, bring him a soda, and cheer. Eventually, he made national news. If you can make directing traffic fun to do and exciting to watch, you can probably make almost any job special.

Adding an element of music, dancing, humor, or kindness can make something that would have been dull, or anxiety provoking, potentially interesting. We do best, however, when we already are spending significant time doing things toward which we naturally gravitate. It's so important at a young age to be *exposed* to many things but *required* to do very few. We are not failing as parents if our children do not find every subject in school fascinating all the time and do not accomplish the same things that we did at their age or that some of their peers do. What is important is that our kids search until they find work that taps into their deepest passions.

If our children can begin finding those strengths and interests early, they will be happier and more successful. Studies consistently show they will even reap the health benefits of being happy from things that naturally motivate them and avoid the many negative effects that come from frustration and depression.[27] In addition, when our kids have a passion for something, they will be able to get started, even when conditions are less than optimal. Being enthused gives them extra energy, in effect giving them more hours in the day to get things done. This kind of drive is valued by teachers and employers alike, who see greater productivity and appreciate what they will characterize as a positive attitude. Also, when our kids are enthusiastic, they do more interesting things and are more likely to draw people to them who are also excited about their lives. It's like being famous or super good looking (not speaking from personal experience); everybody wants to be around you. Finally, you'll enjoy

---

[27] Rimer, "The Biology of Emotion."

your children more if they are happily pursuing what they love. Enthusiasm and happiness are contagious in the best of ways.

☼ Something to Try . . . Find a Local Model

Whenever the opportunity arises, speak with admiration about people who love their work and do it well. Try to go beyond the very famous and the well compensated. Look for local heroes and heroines—an owner of a local store, the person who organized a local 5k race for a charity, a teacher's aide who is fully invested in the kids and does a great job. See if your child notices both the range of people, in terms of personalities and areas of focus, and the commonalities: a certain focus and flow in everything they do. We want this for our kids—to commit to things in which they can become immersed, where they can make a difference, and where they can achieve their potential.

Chapter 2

Winning Approaches:
How Parents Can Facilitate Change

Correction does much, but encouragement does more.

—Johann Wolfgang von Goethe

Introduction: Considerations Before Jumping In

When our children are doing what we want and we do not need to exert a great deal of effort, it can be very gratifying. Whatever we are doing as parents seems to be working, at least from our point of view. We feel that we're pretty good parents, that our kids are going to be okay, and that the difficult times we had were worth it. When our children aren't doing what we want them to do, we start getting concerned.

Although I made the case in chapter 1 that our children deserve to have their own opinions and to make important choices, sometimes our children's poor choices are more consequential than wearing an unflattering outfit to school or staying up a bit late one night because of poor planning and time management. Sometimes, we have valid reasons to be concerned about our kids and to try our best to influence them.

The framework and strategies provided in this chapter are effective for helping our children change when our instinctual responses, such as scolding or threatening, will not work. However, just as we have to be judicious about when to exercise power in a direct and obvious manner—through threats, punishments, rewards, bribes, and so forth—it's also important to have some criteria in deciding when we want to influence our children in more clever and subtle ways. When does "being the adult" force us to give it our very best shot to influence the direction our children take? Is it for matters of safety only? What about personal hygiene? How about their personal relationships and social skills? Their work habits? Their helpfulness around the house? Does it include forcing our children to take advantage of opportunities?

There are plenty of battles not worth fighting at all and others that clearly require us to be heavy handed or to simply make the decision and inform our children. This chapter shows how to be effective when a lighter touch is the best approach, one that uses persuasion instead of coercion and that, at its root, focuses on strengthening the relationship and moving our children toward independence.

Put the R Before the T: Building a Foundation

This chapter will focus its efforts on helping you to reach your child before you begin to teach them. In the helping professions, veterans often say: "R comes before T." This expression means that a solid relationship must exist before we can focus on getting our clients or patients to accomplish tasks. My coaching company, Beyond BookSmart, has developed a methodology to accomplish just this.

With this process, known as "Reach, Teach, Reflect, Release," we also put the "R" before the "T," knowing we must reach children before we can teach them. Likewise, as parents trying to build our children's skills, we need to begin by building our relationships with them. Building the relationship requires time, discipline, insight, and wisdom. Making these investments in the relationship is not just a nice thing to do but extremely pragmatic. It gives us leverage and puts money in the relationship bank account.

It's important to begin with the caveat that some of the things we must do to strengthen our relationships with our children will not yield immediate payoffs. In fact, if you read the fine print in the parenting handbook they gave you when your child arrived at your door, the only result we may get at times is an eye-roll. Overlooking the sassiness is easier when we remind ourselves that we are playing the long game. We are doing things that will help our children become happy and successful; even if they're not constantly thanking us, there's a fair chance that they will later if we've done the best we can. In fact, they may notice and appreciate our efforts along the way, even if they don't come right out and tell us so. This chapter aims to provide guidance *about* guidance, about how we can offer support to our children in a way that will be effective.

The first element needed is time. Spending quality time with our children is a prerequisite to having influence on them. Spending time shows them that we care. If we are too busy because of work or other obligations—even reasonable ones such as caring for our own parents or working crazy hours—we need to level with them about our limitations, and we also have to make the most of the time that we do have with them. We have to be present during that time, not distracted by our computers and our phones and our various adult worries. Imagine how attentive you would likely be if you managed to get time with a celebrity that you greatly admired; try to give at least half of that level of attention to your child for just five minutes a day. Make your children feel famous to *you*, that there is nothing you'd rather be doing during that time than being with them. Knowing they are valued puts a lot of money in the relationship bank account with them.

Another key component is self-discipline, the discipline it takes to override our emotions and conditioning to make smart, kind decisions, especially when we're dealing with stressful situations involving our children. Prior to having my own children, I could not have had the empathy needed to write this section. The most honest thing I can say now is OMG (insert your own emoji here, if you know what I mean)! It is a lot of work sometimes. A metaphor inspired by one of my mentors will help here. It takes a lot of puffs to fill a balloon, but just one aggressive move to pop it. Therefore, difficult as it is, we have to minimize what at times may be our natural inclination toward judgment, sarcasm, threats, bribes, punishments, and other harsh tools that seem to be our only options when we're tired and frustrated. We need to keep in mind that every action of ours makes a difference to our kids and to our relationship with them; unfortunately, those types of behaviors make the wrong kind of difference! They cloud our thinking, damage our children's trust in us, and hurt our children's chances of becoming thoughtful, self-motivated adults.

On the other hand, when we consciously choose the long-term benefits of being disciplined over the immediate gratification of surrendering to our frustration, we serve as role models for our children, strengthen our own self-discipline, and cement their trust in us. Fortunately, we don't have to have a perfect score. What matters is the percentage of time that we are patient and our ability to stop ourselves with a "self-time-out." While we all make mistakes, we can use this discipline to prevent ourselves from going completely off the rails. Just as importantly, when we do screw up with a harsh comment or a judgment or an idle threat, we can recover with a heartfelt apology. Discipline is mostly about prevention, but it's also about recovery.

Sometimes, having a simple, reliable refrain can help. Jim and Charles Fay, who developed the Love and Logic parent courses, have a nice quip: "I love you too much to argue."[28] Through the use of phrases like that, we can remind our children that we care even if we can't come up with a clever reply in the moment when our brains may not be functioning at their very best. An educator friend of mine, Sheryl Seef, has changed the saying "You get what you get, and you don't get upset," to "you might get upset." How powerful! By changing just one word, we can transform our message to be empathic instead of demanding and judgmental, and we still get to encourage the kind of maturity needed to succeed in life. "You get what you get and you might get upset, and I care how you feel . . . but you'll be okay" is the message.

Having some ready statements such as these prevents us from just saying whatever the heck we're thinking. Sometimes, having something good at the ready is better than just "being ourselves." If being ourselves means being reactive, then being prepared means being better versions of ourselves. Being skilled at responding to the trials and tribulations we will inevitably face as parents, having a general openness to our children, and being genuinely interested in their lives creates a foundation that makes them want to stay connected to us even as they mature and need us less.

Something to Try . . . When You Want Your Child to Open Up to You

The next time your child offers to share something with you, ask them what else they'd like to tell you about it. Keep going, maintaining your interest, until your child is done. If you have a judgment

---

28 Fay, "Two Ways to Neutralize."

about whether this thing they're sharing is good or bad, don't say so. Just consider the possibility that your opinion may be irrelevant to what your child needs right now. If you have a suggestion for how they could do more with it, refrain. Simply notice that your child is sharing something. This exercise is a real challenge, but it builds our skills at both placing focused attention on our child and at having the discipline not to act on our impulses.

The Adult in the Room: Managing Our Own Pesky Emotions

I figured that as a professional who has worked with delinquent kids in the woods, taught in the suburbs, run a school in a small city, and coached students over the past two and a half decades, I would have practiced managing my own feelings enough to be able to put my needs aside when taking care of kids. However, even though I love them the most, being consistently calm and supportive for my *own* children can still be the biggest challenge of all. Even when they're relatively easy, it's always hardest with our own kids for three reasons:

- We interact with them more than we do with other people's children.

- They see us when we're not in public and not at our best.

- We are even more invested in their being successful and happy than we are in other children. We get more emotional because we care even more.

These feelings can be rather powerful, and their effects can be detrimental if we don't manage them effectively. Without thinking about it, we may find ourselves yelling at our children to change their tone of voice (hmmm), comparing our children to one another to shame one of them into getting motivated (really?), or predicting their future demise if they don't get on the ball (not inspiring!). Sometimes, we do these things knowing we are screwing things up, but, under pressure, we get desperate and do it anyway.

When we are governed by our emotions, particularly our fears, we drive our kids away from us, making it more likely that the very things we are trying to prevent will occur. This is why the ability to put our own emotions aside, while so difficult, is so important. Our kids' feelings need to be addressed first, even when we're feeling stressed out, disappointed, or hurt. We have to aim to be the adults in managing our own feelings when our kids may not yet have the skills to manage theirs.

My own experience with kids, both personally and professionally, is that the adage "You need to give respect in order to get it" is true. It has always seemed unreasonable to demand that either my students or my own children treat me with respect before I give it to them. It is faster, easier, and more logical for me to be the one to give it first. I don't mean that we should be deferential to children, and we certainly shouldn't be afraid of them. By "respectful," I mean that we take a genuine interest in their perspectives and state our opinions without condescension. Then, when we need to impose our decisions because we do know better and are charged with caring for our kids, we do so mindfully; we're not trying to change their feelings, just their behavior. It may be necessary to put limits on the phone, but they don't also need a lecture, or to be told that they have no right to be upset.

When we don't lead with respect, when we insist that they treat us with respect first, they're definitely not going to *feel* respectful toward us, even if they fake it out of concern for the consequences. At times, getting good behavior without their allegiance may be necessary, but it's a short-term victory. Forcing them to behave without any buy-in certainly doesn't generate a feeling of gratitude or admiration for us, and, for many children, it will make them act out more.

If we lead by being positive and courteous toward our children, reciprocation is far more likely. While there are certainly a few who will mistake kindness for weakness, most won't, especially if we level with them. We can ask, if they seem to be pushing limits and being disrespectful, "Is there something that would explain your tone of voice? I can't see what I've done to deserve it." Often, the response is, "No, I'm just frustrated about" whatever it is. It may be something on their mind about a friend or school. It may actually be something to do with us, and that can be tremendously enlightening. Now there's a chance to talk about it. We now have a chance to strengthen the relationship.

Father Knows Best? Keeping Our Egos in Check

In *The Prophet,* the poet Kahlil Gibran writes, "Your children are not your children. You may give them your love but not your thoughts for they have their own thoughts."[29] Our job, he says, is to be sturdy, stable, and pliable like a bow so that we can launch them in the direction that they choose.

As our children grow, our challenge is to shift from directing them, to advising them, to simply cheering and supporting them from the sidelines. I have worked with many families whose kids have particular struggles—learning disabilities, ADHD, mental health issues—that make it even harder for the parents to know just how

---

[29] Gibran, *The Prophet.*

much to let go and how much to stay involved. Many of them try so hard to strike the right balance for their children, knowing that what was helpful for one child may not be effective for another, and what may have helped a child survive certain challenges when they were younger will only serve to stifle their growth as they get older. It can be difficult to adjust our parenting styles as our children grow; but when we allow them to make mistakes and learn from them, and accept that we don't have the final word on what direction our children's lives will go, our children do a better job of forming their own identities.

That's easier said than done. One dad, whose son I used to work with, kept telling me that he knew what his son needed to do to get his act together because the son, according to the dad, was "just like me!" Actually, the son was just like himself, not his dad. I knew the dad and the son and liked them both. They did have some things in common—not just their last names, but also an energy and an excitement about discussing sports, and an aversion to most academically oriented work. They also had tremendous differences. The son was a good listener, friendly, and fairly content. The father was a talker, slightly aggressive, and super ambitious. The dad's insistence that he knew what his son needed because the son was just like him blinded him to seeing who his child was. The dad became more rigid about what his son should do and often forced unadvisable recommendations on him. Not surprisingly, the son chose a path of rebellion and self-destruction that was far more intense than it needed to be, given the son's naturally amiable disposition.

Because we, as adults, know that we have thought through our values, it can be easy to assume that if our children simply adopted those values and the goals we have for them and did their utmost to achieve them, then they would be successful and happy. That logic doesn't really work, though. My own father was a gifted surgeon, but I don't have his incredible eyesight or steady hands. I also don't find it attractive to dig into people's tendons and whatever else lies under the skin. Our children can respect us but still choose their own paths.

A proposition more likely to succeed and far easier to do than creating a "Mini-Me" is for us to model being true to ourselves as we encourage our children to figure out their own set of values. In doing so, we establish credibility. Since we have mastered ourselves, we are in a good position to be a resource for our children when they have questions. We can offer support and sometimes advice as they figure out who *they* want to be. Moreover, if they are trying to grow into their own best selves, into the adults they want to be, they will need to have both the means to figure out solutions for themselves and the motivation to want to get there.

Something to Try ... When You Disagree with Your Child

The more that we allow our children to become who they feel they need to be, the more willing they will be to share with us. And the interesting paradox is that the more they feel valued for being themselves, the more they will allow us to influence them. Consider something your child says they would like to do that you don't support. It could be something small, such as participating in a certain extracurricular activity, or something big, such as a possible career choice. Notice all of your reasons for objecting: It's too dangerous, it's not practical and won't pay the bills, nobody makes it in that field, it's a waste of your child's talent, it's too hard, it's too easy.

Now consider the other side, your child's perspective. What do you think the draw is for your child? What are the motives? Can you relate to the motives even if you can't understand this particular interest? What would happen if you focused on endorsing your child's enthusiasm without endorsing that particular application? Would it be possible to be honest without being judgmental? What would happen if you said, "I'm not sure how I feel about this whole [insert topic here] thing, but I love your excitement about it. How can I help?"

Stages of Change: An Overview

So, having established that we're comfortable letting our children have a good amount of self-determination, we also know that we play a crucial role in their growth. Especially when we see them heading in a direction that concerns us, it's important for us to intervene. Sometimes, though, if we find our efforts are ineffective, we wonder whether our children really can change.

It's helpful to look into our own experiences of trying to overcome inertia, negative habits, and strong feelings, to answer that. If our own belief system is that nobody really changes, at least not for the better, then it will be that much harder to see when our children make positive changes. We may not recognize what change looks like, waiting for something huge and obvious, even though the signs may be subtle for a while. We may get discouraged because results aren't happening quickly enough, or because we see ourselves or our children slipping backward at times.

Whether it's quitting smoking, exercising more, or doing better in school, it's hard to change. Our current behavior is invariably the easier course to take: We're just doing what we usually do, what's comfortable, what requires little effort. We need significant courage and force of will to change, and when it comes to assisting our kids, it requires us to be far more skillful than comes naturally to most of us. A bit of worthwhile marriage advice that applies to our parenting, too, is: "Don't just 'be yourself.' Be someone a little bit better."

Adopting a new perspective and making changes takes effort. What complicates the process further is that the change we seek is not always the change we see. Change happens incrementally, in ways that are typically not visible for some time. As a result, we don't always see that we or our children are making progress, so we can get unnecessarily discouraged.

A helpful perspective comes from the work of Dr. James Prochaska and his colleagues, who developed the Transtheoretical Model of Change.[30] They discovered several stages people go through in adopting new behaviors for long-term change. Understanding these stages can allow those of us who want to help, including parents, have a better idea of what to do and say to be more supportive and to facilitate change, or at least not to impede it. In breaking out of established patterns to make positive changes in our lives, people proceed through several stages. Understanding these stages confers two major benefits. First, as noted, it can allow us to be more patient, optimistic, and committed in the process. Second, if we know the stage someone is in, we can choose a way to help them that makes sense for that particular stage. Someone who is just beginning to think about making a change, for example, would not be well-served with a "hop right to it" approach from a well-meaning friend or parent. They'd need patience and support.

The work of Prochaska and his colleagues and the research of his team have been endorsed worldwide by medical schools, the American Cancer Society, and numerous other highly regarded organizations. The strategies his team researched serve as the foundation for the work my company does to make sure we take the right approach, based on the student's mindset. In our work with

---

[30] Prochaska, Norcross, and DiClemente, *Changing for Good*. See also James and Janice Prochaska's *Changing to Thrive*.

thousands of students for more than a decade, we have found that it is vital to assess accurately the stage someone is in before trying to help them make a change. Even if we mean well, if our approach is not in sync with where the person is in the change process, we won't have much of an impact. Imagine a relay race where you are carrying a baton and need to hand it off to the next runner—who happens to be your child. You have to slow down and let your child gain a little speed to find that matching point where the two of you are at the same pace and able to make the hand-off.

What follows is a description of the stages, so you can have a sense of how ready your child is to tackle a task, whether it's studying for a math exam or cleaning their room, revising a science lab or getting along better with siblings, planning out an essay for English or getting prepared for college applications. These stages are Precontemplation, Contemplation, Preparation, Action, and Maintenance, and are explained in detail below.[31] The behaviors and attitudes cut across domains and include—but certainly go beyond—schoolwork. It takes practice to become comfortable with and effective at guiding others to shift from one stage to another, but it's not necessary to be a professional to be helpful. In fact, even knowing what the stages are will have an immediate impact, as it will help you to frame your child's struggle as a process and to see that where they are today is a stage, not a final state. By easing the pressure of having to solve a problem immediately, we exit the crisis mentality of having to save our kids from imminent disaster. Instead, we can reframe our role as calm guides who are helping to support a longer-term transformation.

---

[31] A final stage called Termination is used for clinical work helping patients. In our coaching practice, we call it Graduation.

Stage 1. Precontemplation: How to Talk . . . When Kids Won't Listen[32]

In the first stage of change, which is known as Precontemplation, the person is not yet even considering making a change. In this case, your child is not running at your speed and ready for the hand-off. In fact, your child is sitting in the locker room and refusing to come out to the track for the meet. They may be saying they want to quit the "stupid" team.

For schoolwork, Precontemplation can range from extreme opposition—refusal to go to school, or knock-down fights about starting homework—to the quieter but still concerning situation in which your child denies that anything is wrong, but you know that they are lost in their classes and have, more or less, given up.[33] If your child is in the Precontemplation stage, he or she is likely to say how "impossible" or "unfair" the assignments are, and to say, "I can't do it" or "I'm not going to do that!" When people are at this stage, it is pointless to argue with them, as they are not *intellectually* opposed to making a change; they are *emotionally* opposed.

Therefore, persuading them with logic about why they should change their minds is not possible. They are more likely to blame us for making a big deal out of "nothing" than they are to thank us for noticing that they are struggling. In fact, our efforts will actually make the situation worse and will lead to them opposing *us* as well as the work. It bears repeating that they are not intellectually opposed to doing something; they are emotionally opposed. If we miss that distinction and try to engage in a rational conversation, assuming we can persuade them to do things differently, all of our

---

[32] This subtitle alludes to the wonderful book *How to Talk So Kids Will Listen and Listen So Kids Will Talk,* by Adele Faber and Elaine Mazlish.
[33] See Peter Gray, "How Does School Wound?"

efforts will fail to help. Instead, we must begin where our children are, and that means asking questions and genuinely listening to their responses. Once we have a good idea of what is really bothering them—whether it's a teacher, a kid in their class, the content, or knowing how to study—we can begin identifying a specific path to address their concerns.

In general, the place to begin is both simple and hard: being emotionally supportive. This step precedes addressing their stated concerns because they initially might not tell us what is really bothering them. In fact, they may not even know why they are so resistant until they've blown off some steam. As difficult as it is to let our kids be irrational, it's usually necessary. Once they've had a chance to talk about "how much the teacher hates them" or "how stupid the assignment is," we can go to the next level.

Beyond simply listening to their complaints, we can find a way to relate to them and show empathy. Showing empathy doesn't mean agreeing with them. Rather, it means relating to their feeling. In this case, saying, "Yep, I remember courses when I was in school where I couldn't figure out why I had to learn something. Like, why would I ever need to know some of the chemistry we were learning when I wanted to be a lawyer!" Our kids are usually relieved to know that we experienced real frustration as children and that we understand their feelings. By keeping it focused on the same type of frustration—in this example, about having to deal with what feels like irrelevant nonsense—they know that we really "get it."

That opens the door to another technique, which is empowering them. At its most basic level, this means accepting the reality that this young person will be deciding what to do about the situation. Our preferences are not the focus. Young people in any stage of the change process appreciate the chance to make their own decisions, but for those in Precontemplation who aren't even considering a change yet, it is absolutely imperative. They need to have that power even though we may really cringe at the decisions they make.

Of course, this type of acceptance could, at times, lead to your child saying, "My call is to not do my homework." How do we respond to that? We prove that we weren't manipulating them earlier by letting them know that it is their decision. "Honey, I understand. Let me know if you think I could be of any help with it. I have ideas, but it seems too frustrating to have you take it on right now." We double down on the empathy, normalization, and empowerment, and they have to decide whether to open the door at all. In most cases, over time, they will shift to the next stage, Contemplation, simply because they have come to trust us.

Knocking Before Entering: How to Know When to Talk[34]

When we offer to help our children, we need to bear in mind an important caveat. We need to see if they are receptive before we try too hard to persuade them to do what we think is best. Before we offer any specific advice, we need to see if they are even interested in the help to begin with. Even if they say they want our assistance, we need to be somewhat cautious in our delivery. For example, if we show our children how to do something, and they tell us that we're doing it incorrectly, we may feel tempted to let them know that we don't like their attitude. Unfortunately, when we do this, we lose their engagement and trust. They will now focus on us being a "pain" or "not getting it," and not on the homework itself. To some extent, this diversion is something our homework-avoidant kids may actually want, since it's easier to get frustrated with us than to get the work

---

[34] See Kegan and Lahey, *How the Way We Talk Can Change the Way We Work.*

done. We can break that pattern. Instead of correcting them by saying, "I actually have it right. It's *you* who has it wrong," we can ask them, "It's not right? Why not?"

We can let them explain. In doing so, we're getting them to think and take ownership. If we let them explain, and they do happen to know something we don't—for example, an alternate approach explained by the teacher—the good news is that we'll have saved ourselves the embarrassment of being proven wrong. We will also have allowed our children to apply what they have learned. (In fact, as a teacher, I would deliberately make mistakes and let the class correct me. It inspired a level of attention I could rarely get otherwise.) On the other hand, if they are indeed mistaken, we don't have to agree with them, but they'll have had the chance to speak their views aloud and may even notice their mistakes in the process. That's still a good outcome. Finally, if they *still* don't notice, we let them decide whether to accept our help.

We can knock again, as with, "Would you like my thoughts on it? I'm happy to help."

If we get a "no," it may feel bad to let them turn in an assignment with errors, but we are absolved of our responsibility for that night's homework. Hooray! It's our child's choice, and if they do poorly, they may come to realize that they have us as free consultants who are happy to help. Whether they eventually decide to take us up on our offer is a complex algorithm, having something to do with our level of humility, their level of confidence, how desperate their situation is, and how confident they are in our ability to help. However, if we start with humbly offering to help, the odds of our children taking advantage of our assistance go up dramatically. If our children do say "yes," that's even better. We have the opportunity to teach a bit. This "knock first" approach is especially critical for those in Precontemplation.

> ### Something to Try . . . When Setting the Stage for a Challenging Conversation

Try to remember if your own parents ever offered unwanted advice, and then try "knocking before entering" with your child. Especially if you are bringing up a concern that you expect your child will not want to discuss, ask if it is a good time to talk. If they says it's not, ask when it will be. If you get a "when hell freezes over" kind of answer but the topic needs to be addressed, then, within reason, allow them to choose the time and place. You're letting them win on the details of where and when, so you can win on the big picture of addressing the concern. Of course, this is their win, too, since you are having the conversation for their benefit.

Stage 2. Contemplation: How to Encourage an Ambivalent Kid

If your child is somewhat open to making changes but has not committed to it, they are in the stage known as Contemplation. To continue with the race analogy, your child is now observing the relay races. Perhaps they'll participate in the race, perhaps not. To do, or not to do—that is the question. What is common at this stage is to hear comments like, "Yeah that's probably a good idea," or "I could do that, but . . ."

What is happening here is that our kids have not yet found sufficient motivation or confidence to overcome their inertia. While they are beginning to realize some of the potential negatives of their behavior and are now less anxious and frustrated, they are still ambivalent. They know that making a change is probably for the best, but they are also put off by the extra effort required, especially without a guarantee of success.

In addition, they may or may not be aware of the more complex ramifications that may be holding them back.[35] For example, they may be worried about failing and the embarrassment they will feel if they actually try. They may worry that success will put pressure on them to continue succeeding, a pressure they do not currently feel, since they are not trying. There are many reasons why our kids can get stuck in the Contemplation stage for a long time. Because of this ambivalence, because they are not entirely motivated, our kids also remain vulnerable to distractions.

Still, this stage is a considerable step forward from the previous stage, in which they refused to consider the possibility of doing things differently. We do not need to be quite as delicate with them in this stage as we were when they were emotionally triggered. We can encourage, we can teach, and we can challenge them a bit when they have reached this stage. Unlike those in the Precontemplation stage, people in the Contemplation stage are willing to have a conversation about whether or not to change. When our children are stuck here, the exercise ahead in figure 5 can help them see why changing any major habit—with regards to homework, extracurriculars, exercise or something else—makes sense. Doing this sort of exercise can generate a shift in mindset and an infusion of energy that our kids will need as they move into Preparation.

Something to Try . . . When You Want Your Child to Reconsider a Decision

Ask your child for a good time to talk through something on your mind. The conversation is not optional, but the time and place are.

---

[35] For the single best treatment I've seen on resolving ambivalence, see the work of Robert Kegan and Lisa Lahey on our "immunity to change." Harvard Extension School, "The Surprising Reason We Don't Keep Our Resolutions."

Having the chat over an ice cream might not be a bad idea . . . Begin by confirming that they are indeed somewhat open to changing a certain behavior (how they study for tests, whether they go in for extra help, and so forth). If you get an "I guess," you're on the right track. If you get outright opposition, abandon this exercise and go back to the previous section on Precontemplation. If you get considerably more enthusiasm, well, you can continue (at least with the ice cream), but your child may already have advanced to the next stage, which is Preparation.

Assuming that you've got it right, that your child is fairly open to making a change but also not yet committed to it, make a four square Decisional Balance Sheet (see figure 5 for an example of one we did with one of our students) to walk them through the pros and cons of both making a change and doing things the way they currently do. The order matters:

Step 1. Pros of staying the same
Step 2. Cons of staying the same
Step 3. Cons of making a change
Step 4. Pros of making a change

It's important to begin with the pros of staying the same, as that prevents the person from feeling forced into changing their mind. Then, looking at the cons of staying the same is next; they will perceive this as reasonable, even expected. Since your child is in Contemplation, not Precontemplation (and so not emotionally opposed), they will likely go along with this step. Step 3 is an easy sell, listing the cons of changing. Your child will be surprised to have this opportunity to list all the reasons why they should *not* put in more work, not try to be more effective, and so forth. It's fun to be contrary. Feel free to participate, especially by adding in slightly ridiculous reasons that make them laugh. The final step, step 4, is to list the pros of changing. It's best to let your child lead here and to ask permission to add your own. You don't want to seem too enthusiastic, or the entire activity will feel manipulative. While we may hope that our kids will yell "Eureka!" and decide to make the change right then and there, it's more likely that this exercise will be part of a gradual shift. It will take some back and forth before they finally settle into the real decision to start now. At that point, they have shifted to the next stage, Preparation.

SAMPLE

Define the issue: My Gaming Habits	
Step 1—Benefits/Advantages of things staying the same:	**Step 2—Costs/Not so good things about things staying the same:**
• helps me relax • something to do with friends • fun	• up really late playing • hard to stop playing most of the time • don't want to try other things or meet new people (like to stay in)
Step 3—Costs/Not so good things about changing:	**Step 4—Benefits/Advantages of changing:**
• won't have a way to de-stress • hard to hang out with friends if I don't play • I'll get bored • too expensive to go out	• probably get more sleep • easier to get to class if I don't play in morning • get out of my room more • could meet new people?

Figure 5: Decisional Balance Sheet Sample

Stage 3. Preparation: How to Assist When Your Child Is Ready

In both Preparation and the stage after it, Action, students shift from examining the possibility of change to embracing it. The runner is stretching, looking at what is coming up, judging how fast they will need to go, making sure their laces are tied, and providing positive messages to themselves about their ability to succeed.

At school, they are not deciding whether or not they are going to try. They are taking every possible precaution to ensure success: learning necessary skills, acquiring resources, making a plan, and engaging others as supports. The teacher can sense it in the room when students are motivated and have advanced past Contemplation. Teachers and parents alike can sense the optimism that the kids feel as they get ready to implement real changes.

Parents are very happy when their kids reach the Preparation stage. When kids enter this stage, they are clearly motivated. Now, they are receptive to advice, sometimes—wait for it—even to their own parents' advice! Yes, our egos finally get a tip of the hat. Even more gratifyingly, we can see more tangible evidence of the changes our children are making. They are doing things that we believe will make a difference in their lives. We not only hope but see that they're doing well, and can believe that they are going to be okay without us at some point. We see that they have learned from challenges and mistakes, that they are resilient, and, especially, that they can motivate themselves even for things they're not excited about but that are necessary. They seem more focused as well, able to remove unnecessary distractions. Overall, they seem more mature and perhaps capable of doing well in the Age of Attention.

It is important to note that this stage is on the heels of, but not exactly the same as, the next stage, Action. This stage is about gathering everything that will be needed for the job, whether it's a mundane task, such as, literally, sharpening pencils or gathering materials, or something more involved, such as making a plan to get a project done or identifying the support network needed to sustain the effort to come. The next stage is about putting those sharpened pencils to paper.

Something to Try . . . If Your Child Is Not Anticipating the Likely Challenges Ahead

Ask your child how they feel now about beginning the challenge that they are working on. At this point, you ought to hear excitement and curiosity about starting. One thing you may not yet notice is a sense of determination and persistence about finishing. This phase, Preparation, seems to generate a good deal of energy about beginning but not necessarily completing things. Therefore, since setbacks and challenges are inevitable, the goal here is to anticipate and prevent as many of the problems as possible. This stage is an excellent time for your child to be intellectually engaged and to envision the possible obstacles, including the tendency people have to quit when the going gets tough.

Potential Problem	Likelihood	Level of Concern	Action Plan
Example: Forgetting to check project planner	Somewhat	Huge deal!	Multiple calendar alerts

Figure 6: Managing Potential Problems Before Shifting to Action

Work with your child to generate a list of these possible problems (see figure 6). Rate them twice—once for how likely they are to occur (very likely, somewhat likely, unlikely) and once for how problematic they'd be (huge deal, moderate deal, not a big deal). For the ones that would be a huge deal and are at least somewhat likely to occur, have a very concrete plan in place for what to do about them. For those that pose a moderate problem and are also moderately or very likely to occur, have a basic idea of how to identify the problem and what the first steps will be in response. Being proactive like this will give you and your child a sense of confidence that the hard work to come will not suddenly be lost. You have a plan for what you will do. There's also a second benefit: Simply having this response plan makes it less likely you'll even need it.

Stage 4. Action: Getting Out of the Way of a Kid in Motion

All of this work in Preparation paves the way for the transition to Action, the stage where your child accelerates their speed, receives the baton and runs independently, maintaining their best pace and completing the task to the best of their ability. A moment ago, our children were focused on their checklists of what must be done and buoying themselves up for the big start, saying things like, "I can't wait to . . ." or "I'm going to." In Action, they are tightly focused on the task at hand, relatively free of self-talk. If they are saying anything to themselves, it is primarily action-oriented, as in "Do this, not that. Back to the task," without the excitement of Preparation, the doubt of Contemplation, nor the pain and despair of Precontemplation. At this stage, our kids have built up a certain immunity to the distractions around them. Whatever their baseline was, they can now focus their attention on priorities much more easily.

It often takes considerably more time and effort to arrive at the Action stage than either we or our children expect. The problem with underestimating the length and ruggedness of this journey is that it leads to quitting. People often expect that they or their children can simply jump straight to the Action stage and are then shocked to discover how unrealistic they had been. When our kids are stuck, we are tempted to dive in with short-term solutions because we want to see results ASAP, but changes only endure when the earlier hard work has already been done. Facing the resistance of Precontemplation, understanding how change occurs and wrestling with self-doubt in Contemplation, and gathering resources in Preparation are all meaningful and necessary steps along the way.

For precisely this reason, New Year's resolutions almost always fail, as do crash weight-loss programs and other quick fixes. Like a runner who wants to complete the race but hasn't trained properly, students will not sustain the changes they make, academic or otherwise, unless they have organized themselves and mentally prepared for the challenging course ahead.

Something to Try . . . When Making Multiple Changes at Once Seems Like a Bright Idea

List three things you'd like to accomplish or change in your own life at some point. What stage are you in for each of the three? Could you confidently be at the Action stage for any one of them by next week? How about all three of them? Would you rather change all three of them at once or just work on one at a time?

While this book is primarily about helping our kids, it is, of course, about us as well—whether we are parents or professionals working with children. Doing this exercise can remind us that our children may not necessarily be unwilling to make an immediate change but may simply not be ready to jump into the Action stage at this moment, and certainly not for multiple goals simultaneously.

Stage 5. Maintenance: How to Manage the Inevitable Setbacks

Wonderfully, there comes a time when our children have developed sufficient momentum over a period of time that they really own a new, positive habit. Even if they have a lapse, they understand what it takes to get back on track and have built enough discipline to do so. This recovery process is facilitated by actual changes in the brain that occur from developing expertise and experience, with stronger connections being formed that make these new behaviors increasingly likely to occur and easier to do. In *The Whole-Brain Child*, Drs. Daniel Siegel and Tina Payne-Bryson note that "neurons that fire together wire together," meaning that the nerve cells in the brain that operate consistently in tandem do so more and more effectively.[36] That process is what allows behaviors, positive or negative, to become habit, and, thus, easier to do.

In addition, as they become more self-aware in the Maintenance stage, children's Executive Function skills often start to blossom. They are more capable of noticing when they are off-track and more able to shift their attention back to their priorities. In this stage, their self-concept has shifted, and they say things like, "I used to . . . but now . . ." or "I'm not lazy anymore," or "I really do this for myself now." Ideally, they even get to the point of realizing that once they have improved in one place, they could also make changes in other dimensions of their lives if they invest the time and energy.

The things to keep an eye on once a habit has taken root are lapses and their evil cousins, relapses. Without letting the semantics distract us from the key points, lapses are moments of falling off—the occasional missed homework assignment, for example—and are to be expected on occasion. Relapses, such as wanting to avoid school

---

[36] Siegel and Payne-Bryson, *The Whole Brain Child*.

altogether, can be caused by a difficult change in one's life that can make a child, or even an adult, feel like giving up and needing to take a break on the hard work of changing. When our kids, or we, use the phrase "deserve a break," it's usually not a good sign. It's typically to justify reverting to a negative habit because we're tired and demoralized.

This is the time for our children to rely on the network of support they built during the Preparation phase and may not have particularly needed in the Action phase. It is needed now. Now is also the time to reconnect to the original reasons of why they made the changes in the first place. Those motives, gently brought back to our attention by friends, family, and appropriate professionals, can help get our children back on track.

It's most helpful if we can understand whether the lapse or relapse is mostly due to our children simply being exhausted, which erodes their willpower, or whether something more serious is going on. If they're just plain tired, let them know how common it is to lose steam and that everyone needs occasional downtime. If they're getting demoralized, don't let them wallow in guilt or blame others. Just let them know that these things happen, remind them to reconnect with what motivated them in the first place, and tell them that life is too short to worry about a bad test score, an off day, or whatever the issue is. Try to figure out what might have happened and what can be learned from the experience and move on. In these situations, it's helpful for us to serve as pragmatic cheerleaders. What we're looking for in the typical course of progress and setbacks is to build resilience, to minimize the extent and duration of the backslide, and to help our child return to their highest stage of change as quickly as possible.

If, on the other hand, we suspect something bigger is going on, it's important to find out. We do not necessarily have to know all the details, but if our children know that we are aware that they are dealing with something significant, then we can provide them support. To begin with, they know that we care and that we are available. In addition, we can offer other sources of support that they might accept, such as a therapist. Having another adult to process that with can be helpful when our children struggle with something that is consuming their energy and focus.

Matching Our Approach: A Nuanced Definition of Progress

Whether we are making a change in our own lives or trying to facilitate a change in others, we will be much more successful if we appreciate the fact that forward movement from one stage to another is, in and of itself, real progress. If our children shift from the "No!" of Precontemplation to the "Maybe" of Contemplation, that is progress. If our children suddenly express a willingness to use an assignment book, but bring it home with some inaccuracies, that is progress over refusing to use any system to track work. Understanding this more nuanced version of progress can renew our patience with, and confidence in, both our children and ourselves. Just as importantly, we can use this understanding to help our children celebrate the progress they are already making long before they have attained the concrete reward of an A or some external marker. If they are feeling defeated, we can show them the trajectory they are on and how much growth they have already achieved.

These stages of change have tremendous implications for how we raise our children. To be effective, it's not just that we need to do the right thing; it's that we have to do the right thing at the right time. Did you know that walnuts are a very healthy food, replete with antioxidants, vitamin E, and omega-3 fats? Can you imagine feeding those healthy walnuts to an infant who cannot yet chew food?

A scary idea, right? On the other hand, imagine offering Gerber's baby food to your teenager. It is healthy food, but it ain't gonna happen. Just as we feed our children differently depending on their age and treat them differently based on their maturity level, we will be more effective if we adjust our approach to helping them based on how ready they are to change.

Sometimes the best approach is a little restraint. Silence can easily be worth a thousand words in these instances. When she was ten years old, my younger daughter, Eliya, told me that she got all of the problems right on a math worksheet. After seeing how many problems she had to do and how surprisingly mindless the assignment was, I nearly expressed my frustration. What went through my head was, "Well, that was a waste of time! Did you learn anything from that assignment? Is this teacher really tuned in?"

Whether my thought was unfair to the teacher or spot on, my criticizing the teacher or the work that my daughter had completed would certainly not have provoked a powerful conversation about the nature of standards. Nor would it have inspired my daughter to be a harder worker. Instead, it would have deflated her. I took a breath and shook off my impulse to push my daughter harder. I decided that, at this moment, the point was not that my child might be getting props for doing something that was, well, kid's stuff. The point was that my daughter was happy to share her success with me. I could take up my concern about the level of push with the teacher at another time if it was that important.

All I said to my daughter was, "Well, you sure have persistence. I bet you were bored sometimes, but you showed that you can work hard even when it's not exactly what you'd like to be doing and get a perfect score!"

She beamed. I beamed at her but also at myself for not screwing it up. This time, I had kept the door open for further sharing.

Sometimes, we can find something good even in something not so good. My daughter wasn't looking for my praise about her math skills, just for my acknowledgment of her tenacity.

> ## ⛭ Something to Try . . . When You're Likely to Be Too Critical

Look for an opportunity to be quiet instead of critical when your child is sharing something with you. Take a situation that would prompt you to make a negative comment, such as observing your child's messy room, backpack, clothing, or homework. See if you can notice your own critical voice, the one inside your head insisting that your opinion is very, very important—the one that tells you that your child simply must hear from you now or will go down a very bad path that will end in all seven sins being committed on a daily basis. Take the quiet moment just to listen, to notice your emotional reaction, the one that your intellect also justifies as being right, and just tolerate the discomfort of not saying anything for sixty seconds. Then, see if there is something positive you can say instead. Breathe calmly and try saying it. If you are so calm that your child looks at you like you have three heads, you have succeeded.

Finding a Cognitive Match: Accommodating Different Learning Styles

I had just finished teaching my math students the process for completing a multi-step problem with the operations done in the proper order. Since this was a class for students who had learning disabilities, I had a special education teacher co-leading the class. She spoke up.

"Mr. Delman, would you mind if I showed the class another way to learn the problem?"

"Of course not," I replied.

She proceeded to redo the problem, neatly and methodically just as I had, but exaggerated her facial expressions to show confusion or understanding and . . . she didn't say a single word! I was stunned and loved observing her method. When she finished, she asked the students to raise their hands if they learned better the way that I had taught it, using a verbal explanation. Some raised their hands. I followed by asking who learned it better the way my co-teacher taught it, by watching and thinking but without words. A bunch of hands went up. Then, I asked who learned it best seeing both of our approaches; nearly all of the students raised their hands.

I share this story because the challenge is not always about reaching a child who is in Precontemplation. Although it is not the focus of this book, and others have done the subject justice, it is important to note that we are sometimes trying to help kids who are excited to learn, but we don't know the best way to reach them intellectually. Unlike kids in Precontemplation who are emotionally opposed to tackling the problem because they don't see or aren't interested in the problem (yet), kids in later stages may be ready as long as we speak their intellectual language.[37] In fact, they may even appear, at first, to be in Precontemplation because they are not responding. However, their lack of response is because they are confused, not because they are opposed.

Being able to use multiple approaches makes us more effective parents, as most of us who have more than one child can attest. What worked for one child may not work for a sibling, and what worked earlier in the year may not work as well right now for the same child! Whether it's the teacher, the subject, the particular assignment, or

---

[37] For some of the most insightful work on this topic, see Howard Gardner's work on multiple intelligences. For a starting point, go to http://multipleintelligencesoasis.org/.

our child's mood, we need to be flexible. In doing so, we are also modeling for our children the benefits of learning to be flexible.

Mexico Is Boring: Using Stubbornness to Teach a Lesson

Back when my older daughter, Jenna, was six years old, and we were visiting my father and step-mother in southern Arizona, I let her know that we were taking a day trip to Mexico. She let *me* know that she didn't want to go, at all. I asked her why and to write down her reasons for not wanting to go, which she summarized in writing just one word, "Boring!" I told her it wasn't a negotiation about whether we'd go or not, but she never had to go again if she had a bad time. I also thanked her in advance for going, knowing that she was opposed, and off we went. While there, she had her hair braided in the street, ate helado (ice cream), and haggled over trinkets. When we returned to the car, I asked her what she thought.

"That was awesome!" she said.

"Want to go back some time?" I asked.

"Yeah!" she said.

And then I asked her to read what she had written earlier. She refused. I insisted, reminding her that she had been so sure that it would be awful and had given me a good deal of grief at the time. Sheepishly, she read the note out loud. I left it at that for the time being, but something happened in that moment. It wasn't that I was right and she was wrong. It was that she saw the potential downside of being close-minded.

Over the following years, she has occasionally resisted new ideas without much of a basis. At those times, if I say "Mexico . . ." she will at least reconsider. While she may not end up agreeing to try it after all and may not change her mind about the issue, she will not simply dismiss it out of hand.

We may or may not be able to change our children's minds in the long run, but in this case, I knew she needed more data to even have a chance of changing her mind. Therefore, instead of fruitlessly trying to convince her, I allowed her to say how she felt and told her that she would have the power to say "no" once she had enough experience to make an educated decision. Sometimes we have to put up with our kids being temporarily upset with us, but we can mollify their feelings by letting them know that they will have the choice next time. That approach will make them more likely to consider our perspectives, an important part of the change process.

Something to Try . . . When Your Child Has a Strong Opinion Without Equally Strong Reasons

If your child is opposing you about something, instead of trying to prove your point ahead of time about how great it will be, tell your child that you really don't know how it will be. Let them know that you are interested in their opinion, especially after they give it a try. Be clear about what the minimum time is for you to consider their opinion to be informed (e.g. tapping her toe across the border of Mexico would not have constituted a valid visit for my daughter). Try capturing some of their hysterically funny strong opinions on your phone's video or voice note or by having them write them down. Save it. Blackmail can be such a powerful tool!

Hating Hawthorne: The Benefit of Suspending Judgment

My student began the session saying, "*The Scarlet Letter* sucks! It is the worst book I have ever read." I doubted that he had read much of it, and I nearly replied with a snarky, "Did you even read past page one?" However, instead of assuming, I inquired, "What makes you say that?" To my surprise, he had an answer, and his first complaint was not that the book was boring, which, as it turns out, was his second concern. As he put it, "To be honest, I didn't read very much. It's so irrelevant—who cares about her having adultery? And it's depressing and extremely repetitive. Plus, it's all description!"

Once I saw that his first complaint was that the book was completely irrelevant—after all, what could an affair in the seventeenth century have to do with this high school junior?—I knew that I could help him. My job wasn't to help him with the vocabulary or breaking down the sentence structure; it was, in this case, necessary to show him why the book even mattered. At that moment, he was not thinking about getting a good grade to maintain his GPA. He was not intellectually opposed; he was emotionally resistant due to his total repulsion to the book. In terms of the stages of change, he was clearly in the Precontemplation category.

I asked him if he wanted to see something kind of cool, and he gave me a non-committal, "Sure. Why not?" I didn't oversell, which helped him shift to Contemplation, enough to begin the conversation. I showed him a couple clips from 60secondrecap.com, a well-crafted series of minute-long tutorials that explain the basic premises behind a number of the classics. After watching them, my student looked at me in surprise and said, "Oh! It's like high school—how everybody judges each other and puts labels on each other. Maybe the book won't be so bad."

Next, I showed him something a neuropsychologist friend of mine calls "speed limits" in reading, a method of assessing the relative importance of different sections of a book and then slowing down appropriately for critical passages and speeding up for parts that are less likely to yield much value.[38] This adjusting to the nature of the text, far from cheating, actually shows a deeper appreciation for the work than if you were to simply muddle through. Between these two tools—one for the quick fix and one for the longer-term payoff—he ended up liking, though not loving, a book that was initially destined to be read only via a SparkNotes summary.

I also let him know that his initial resistance to this book was something I've seen plenty of times with students his age and that it was part of a pattern that he was getting better at moving past fairly quickly. While I wanted to normalize his experience so he wouldn't feel judged, I also wanted to open the door to a conversation about how people change and how he has grown as a student. I explained to him the stages of change that have been the focus of this chapter and let him know that he had progressed to the point where my job now was to kick his butt. He laughed and asked what I meant. I explained that he had toughened up and could handle the feedback, which meant that I wasn't going to take his initial eye-rolling all that seriously, and neither should he. Although he'd still get a feeling of "No way—I will not do this" at times, he would now be able to look at his instinctive reaction and make a choice about whether to give in to it or respond differently.

"In sum," I told him, "by being less reactive, you're more like an adult now." He liked hearing that. Becoming less reactive and valuing that growth is part of the Executive Function skillset. Overcoming his impulse to quit and having the flexibility to zoom out from the

---

[38] David Gleason, author of *At What Cost?*

details of the book to the bigger picture of why it matters were additional examples of how his growing Executive Function skills were allowing him to make greater progress.

At times, our kids, like this student I coached, will present as deeply opposed, as if they are in Precontemplation, when a light touch will reveal that they could be moved to Contemplation fairly easily. Our child may just need to blow off a bit of steam before proceeding. If we react gently, they will not need to fight us. However, if we respond aggressively to their resistance, we will escalate the tension.

We could come back with, "What do you mean you don't like the book? It's a classic! Anyway, school isn't meant to be fun all the time. Quit your complaining! When I was a kid, I'd get a good smack if I complained the way you do. It's your job!" We could, but that might turn someone from being in Contemplation to stepping back to Precontemplation simply because of the resentment they feel. If our children are in Contemplation, they may be ready to consider the pros and cons of doing things differently. By using the Decisional Balance Sheet (see figure 5), by teaching our children how people change, and by providing specific tools and supports, we can help shift our somewhat resistant children into Action.

Something to Try . . . When You Want to Reassure Your Child That It's Normal to Struggle

Another technique, beyond the empathy and empowering strategies discussed earlier, is to normalize our children's experience. Instead of demonstrating that you can relate, the key here is to show that their situation is not odd or unusual. You are reassuring your child that they don't need to add a layer of being anxious or angry with themselves for struggling, that it's "normal" to feel the way they're feeling. Although your child may feel like the only one who doesn't get it, it's undoubtedly not the case. When your child says how he's feeling or how unwilling he is to do something, instead of telling him how that won't help him, actually consider for yourself how normal that probably is for someone his age and let him know you understand that. "I'm betting that lots of kids your age feel that way" lets him know you're not judging him.

It's tricky to get this right because it can come off as dismissive. Saying, "Oh, you're so smart. I'm sure all the kids are struggling with this," could be taken as avoiding their feelings. For this reason, showing a bit of empathy before normalizing tends to work well. Once I have said, "Yep, I get how dumb this assignment seems to be—been there myself with lots of things," I can authentically continue with, "I can imagine that a lot of students are feeling the same way." Without overstating how certain I am about their peers, I can tell my students and children that it's likely, if not guaranteed, that they are not alone in their frustration.

A Spoonful of Sugar: How to Make Anything Relevant

Mark didn't see much value in most of what he was supposed to be learning in school. When I met him in his sophomore year, his grades reflected his lack of ambition, and he had zero interest in having me "help" him. On the other hand, he was a brilliant musician, able to compose lyrics and music for a wide range of genres. Before I began working with him, I purchased his album on iTunes, and at our first meeting, I asked him to teach me something on guitar since I definitely didn't know nearly as much as he did. He showed me some bar chords, and when I asked him how he did it, he laughed.

"Dude," he said, "I just broke it down, one finger at a time, with the minimum movement needed to get you from one step to the next."

"Dude," I replied, "that is a great method. I'm going to use that same method when it comes to our working on essays if that's okay."

He said he'd consider trying the approach on his writing, which, given his initial lack of interest in coaching, was an indication that I'd chosen a good tack, one that showed appreciation for who he was. Weeks later, when he had an essay that required my help, I also drew parallels between the writing of an essay and the writing of a song, connecting his awareness of how popular songs typically have a pattern (intro, verses and choruses, and so on), to how persuasive writing can typically be broken down into a simple formula. Mark stared at me in amazement.

"Seriously! You can just follow a pattern?"

I showed him some simple formulas and acronyms that many teachers use for writing a five-paragraph essay. We practiced. He was impressed because he'd thought that essays, unlike songs, required creative genius and an innate "getting it" on how to organize things. He didn't realize that the skill could be taught. Once I had demystified the process for him, he was much more willing to make an effort.

In addition, by seeing the connection between his favorite topic—music—and another application to which he had an aversion, writing, he saw the possibility of even liking the skill that was more difficult for him. While he did not have a passion for writing essays, engaging him in his domain where he could not only relate but could also teach the teacher made him willing to explore an area where he had always felt disaffected and discouraged. As is noted in *Executive Function in Education*, "Connecting new information to prior knowledge by thinking about why the new information makes sense is a very powerful learning strategy, one that produces huge positive effects on learning."[39] Momentum matters. When we focus first on an area of strength and interest, our kids can overcome the self-doubt, anxiety, and avoidance that would have held them back from tackling a challenge.

Something to Try . . . When Your Child Has to Do a "Boring" Task

Take an area you care about in which your child feels little to no interest because she feels intimidated or bored. Now, try to connect it to something your child loves, as I connected writing music to the writing of an essay for my student. If connections do not easily come to mind, go for a walk, lie down, mumble about the two areas, or play a musical instrument. You are looking for a non-obvious connection, so do something creative instead of sitting at a desk with a notebook or a laptop.

After that, whether you have some ideas or not, you can try Google. For example, if your child loves dance but hates math, you can type in "dance math." You will get "dance mat" offerings because Google thinks you've made a typo, but if you click on "Did you mean 'dance math?'" you can then pull up "teaching math through dance" and get a whole bunch of ideas from Mathinyourfeet.com to "Taking the Leap: Teaching Math Through Dance." Since there are about 12,900,000 results even for this search, you can take advantage of the hard work others have done to connect things that kids often struggle with to things kids love. The rewards are potentially enormous. Learning math, something your child must do, might feel somewhat more tolerable if there is at least some ostensible connection to one of your child's passions.

---

[39] Meltzer, "Teaching Metacognitive Strategies," *Executive Function in Education*, 275.

Assignment Book Blues: How to Negotiate with a Kid

I already knew the answer, but it's my job to ask the question when I first meet with a student.

"What percentage of this coaching arrangement is your idea? What percentage is your parents' idea?"

"That would be zero and one hundred," the new student said to me.

"Well, that puts you squarely in the normal category," I said. "So why are you so unenthusiastic about this?" I asked him.

"Two words," he replied. "Assignment book."

"What's the deal with that?" I asked.

"It's stupid. Everyone keeps telling me to use it, and I don't need to. I'm a sophomore, and I've figured out what works."

"So what works?" I asked, amazed at how clear he was and how easy he was making my job.

"Using the online postings. I can just get the assignments there!" he said.

"In every class? Every night?"

"Pretty much. Every class except English. The teacher there doesn't post most of the time."

"Okay, so what do you do for English?"

"Well, obviously, I use my assignment book for that!" he said.

I managed not to laugh, since it might have been taken the wrong way. His parents thought that he had no system, but he did have one. It just wasn't the system that they believed he needed. The student himself thought he was opposed to using the school's assignment book, but he wasn't. He was only opposed to using it unnecessarily.

Imagine the needless friction between a child and either parents or teachers over this topic. Some students get so dug in that they decide to teach the adults a lesson by writing their assignments in the book but then not doing the homework, just to prove the point that the assignment book is, indeed, a waste of time. Other students, when they find that their parents have locked their phones with a new app due to overuse, spend hours figuring out how to hack into their phones instead of spending minutes getting the work done required to regain their phone privileges! Beating the "system" and outmaneuvering the parents becomes the focus, partly because it's more satisfying than the work and, for some, because it may feel more achievable.

Given that we are in the Age of Attention, our kids have endless distractions, but they usually do not have strong enough Executive Function skills to manage those distractions. They may not even recognize that they need to modify their approach. If we're going to help them focus on things that are difficult, we'll need to do more than just insist ever more firmly that they do things our way. We'll need to understand their specific objections to see if we can address some of their concerns.

"We need to find something that has 100 percent reliability and minimum 'annoyability,'" I told my student at our second session. "You get to decide the method, as long as it works." With that arrangement, we began a productive relationship where we could look for evidence of what was working, instead of just about what he wanted and how his parents wanted something else.

⟨💡⟩ Something to Try . . . When Your Child Says "No"

It's worth reiterating that if our children are resisting our ideas, we ought to find out why that is. Sometimes what we think is simply "obvious" is not obvious to them, and sometimes their opposition is well founded. It helps to keep asking until we really understand where they are coming from. Even if their opposition to our ideas turns out not to have a strong basis, it is still helpful to understand their perspective. Doing so allows us to be clear about why we disagree, shows them that we take them seriously, and opens the door to them considering and adopting our perspective.

What is unlikely to work, however, is telling our children or implying to them that our approaches and ideas are much better than theirs. Asking open-ended questions, such as, "Tell me more," or "What makes you say that?" and "How would that work if you did that?" encourages them to think more critically. It builds valuable Executive Function skills that help them become reflective and effective. If they do, on occasion, acknowledge that we were right, we get bonus points for not saying, "I told you so," and double bonus points if we can compliment them on their having figured it out without injecting any irony or sarcasm. Even when we think, "Yeah, but that was really my idea, not theirs," it's fair to bear in mind that they had to come around to it. They will also feel pride in having made a good decision and be more receptive to our thoughts the next time. These are the true "bonus points."

The Problem with Praise: How to Make Feedback Valuable

We know, at some level, that if we focus on what our kids are doing well, then our children will be more inclined to put in effort, and the more they try, the more they will succeed. Their sustained effort, coupled with reflecting on what is and is not working, is the single greatest predictor of success. For this reason, we are drawn to praise our kids. It can feel good for both them and us to say, "You're doing great!" and "I'm so proud of you!" We see our kids smile, and we know they're feeling good about themselves. Their response also reminds us how important we are to them, since we can affect them so powerfully.

However, and you saw this coming if you read the section title, praise has downsides. First, encouragement can border on the absurd, as in, "Oh, you got 25 percent right on that test! Congratulations! Great start! I'm so proud of you—only 75 percent to go!" Obviously, having that great a deficit does not merit that degree of enthusiasm from a parent, and most children would rather have empathy for the disappointment they are feeling than receive false praise for accomplishing so little. Kids see through false praise and lose trust in us because of it.

Second, research has consistently shown that global praise— "Great job!" for example—weakens motivation, moving it from the joy of doing something well to the pleasure of getting a compliment. It also provides no evidence that we truly mean what we are saying if our praise is vague. Finally, we are not offering honest and clear feedback that allows our children to know what effect their work has on others if we just say "Great job!" It can be a way to pretend we are paying attention and simply offering lip service.

Third, praise with ulterior motives—"You're such a good kid. Can you babysit for us tonight?"—erodes trust even more quickly. We may feel that it's nice of us to give a compliment since we were going to require them to do the chore anyway, but it's more honest and fair to simply say, "I need you to do something for me. I do appreciate it."

Are there no opportunities for praise of any sort? Is it necessarily negative? Not at all. Genuine compliments that are limited in scope can have real value. If you're reviewing your child's start to a paper, and it's got oodles of grammatical errors but has something interesting in it, too, there's nothing wrong with saying, "That introduction really makes me want to read the rest of your paper. I thought that first point was very interesting." The need for good editing can come later, either from you or from the teacher. If you can't find an honest compliment, you can ask an honest question: "So, what are you going for in that introduction?"

After an explanation, you can always at least say, "Thanks for sharing!" and you may be able to add something that expresses both what you appreciate and what is not working for you personally. For example, "Yeah, I can kind of see your point, especially that one sentence right there. I'm not seeing the connection in the one after that, but that might just be me." It's not quite offering advice. Rather, if we show an appreciation for their goals and acknowledge examples of success, our children may give us the space to also acknowledge our confusion on something that did not work as well for us. It becomes a *relatively* weak sentence, one that can be fixed to be as good as the others, as opposed to the focus of our entire conversation and an absolute bad.

The three types of "praise" that have known positive effects are praise about effort, impact, and appreciation of the relationship. The first helps build agency, willpower, and resilience. "I'm impressed by how hard you've worked and how much you care" shows genuine respect and, because of that praise, orients them toward fortitude even in the face of difficult outcomes.

The second shows that we're paying attention and genuinely interested in the person. "Let me hear that second verse again. Yeah, that one just gets me for some reason—I love it. Thanks." The third, unconditional love, shows that the relationship has indeed come before the task, that we're happy to be present and have time with our children, not because of what they are accomplishing or even because of their personality but just because of our love for them. Most kids really take it in when we tell them, "I love spending time with you."

Try noticing when you give global praise and observing the effect on your child. Then, deliberately try the other types of praise—based on their effort, impact on you, or just appreciation for the relationship. Observe the impact of those types. It's also a great conversation to have with your child. Try asking them how they experience the different types of praise.

In Closing: The Parenting Effect

Can we, as parents, make a big difference in how well our children develop their Executive Functioning? Although the brains with which our children are born play an undeniable factor, and some parts of the world in which we raise our kids are outside of our control, we do have an impact, based on how we talk to them, how we teach them, and what outside forces we expose them to.

According to the National Scientific Council on the Developing Child, we can help by teaching skills and reducing our role gradually over time so that our children can learn the skills and build the confidence necessary to take ownership of their lives:

> Environments that foster Executive Functioning are characterized by adult-child relationships (both within and outside the home) that guide children from complete dependence on adult support to gradual assumption of the "executive" role for themselves . . . Enhancing the development of Executive Functioning involves sensitive, responsive caregiving and individualized teaching in the context of situations that require making choices, opportunities for children to direct their own activities with decreasing adult supervision over time, effective

support of early emotion regulation, promotion of sustained joint attention, and the availability of adults who
are not under such pressure that they cannot make time
for children to practice their skills.[40]

Although we can't control everything, we can take charge of
those variables within our reach. Indeed, doing so is in the very job
description of being a parent. The effect of our parenting, for better
and sometimes for worse, is still tremendously important.

Ultimately, and a bit paradoxically, our job is to help now so
that we don't need to later. *Smart But Scattered* authors Peg Dawson
and Richard Guare explain, "While inadequate adult support and
supervision leads to obvious problems, overreliance on adults
assuming the role of the child's frontal lobes also has its drawbacks.
Although environmental modifications, including adult support, are
important tools that can help children with weak executive skills
function successfully, the ultimate goal should be to help children
develop their own executive skills sufficiently, so they can function
independently."[41] And that's really what we're going for, kids who
are going to be okay even when we aren't there 24/7.

---

[40] National Scientific Council on the Developing Child, "Building the 'Brain's Air Traffic
Control' System," 6.
[41] Dawson and Guare, *Executive Skills in Children*, 37.

Chapter 3

Zen and the Art of Self-Regulation: Antidotes for Anxious Kids

90% of top performers are skilled at managing their emotions in times of stress in order to remain calm and in control.

—Travis Bradberry, *Forbes* magazine

Introduction: One Brain, Many Parts

Imagine that you have planned out a lovely vacation. You have the tickets, the time off, and a suitcase with everything you need. You're about to hop in a limo (why not?) to head to the airport when suddenly you get filled with anxiety about all of the things you'll need to do when you return, even though, really, you know intellectually that you'll be okay. You have used great Executive Function skills in planning and organization, but your emotions are running amok and could ruin a wonderful experience.

Humans are complex. With so many different parts to our brains and such a range of functions, it's as if we each have multiple brains inside of our skulls. Whether these various parts work together effectively or not is the biggest factor within our control that determines how our lives will go. When they do, we can achieve at levels that defy what we had imagined possible for ourselves. Our enthusiasm becomes energy, and we harness it well to research, to design, to build, to accomplish, and to invent. When those parts do not communicate effectively or, worse still, are at war with each other, we are constantly filled with doubt, stressed, unable to get motivated. We feel depleted and have trouble thinking clearly. We know how important it is for us as adults to manage the emotions that come and go in the course of a day. Our children, of course, must also be able to manage their emotions. It provides them with the stability to put forth sustained and effective effort.

Thankfully, for those of us who are born with more drive than cool—in other words, those of us who don't naturally let things roll off of us—the skill of managing anxiety and frustration can be learned. While the methods outlined in this chapter take time to learn and must be practiced to become and to remain effective, everyone can improve. I know this not only from my own experience but also as one who has witnessed and helped many others work on their challenges in this domain.

It is also worth noting that while nearly everyone struggles to manage strong emotions at times, it is particularly hard for young people. Facing many challenges for the very first time, they don't have the experience to know that things will be okay, that they'll get over their first break-up, their first teacher who's tough as nails, or their first unkind friend. They don't know that, over time, they will learn how to deal with these sorts of inevitable hurts. In addition, their hormonal swings make it more difficult to take things in stride, just as we have a harder time when we're sleep-deprived.

When it comes to school stresses, the same principles apply. Here, even with children who naturally run anxious, we can, by removing the fear of failure, engage them. With children and teens who experience anxiety, handling the "Reach" phase of our Reach, Teach, Reflect, Release coaching process comes with its own set of guidelines. Just as coaches do, we parents can let our children know that we are available to help, but are not anxious to impose ourselves on them. If they are interested, we can model for them how we would approach the situation, and we can assist in the solutions and transfer responsibility to them at a pace that they can manage. By approaching them in these non-judgmental ways and using what we've learned about the stages of change, we help them build this critical skill of emotional self-management and attain the confidence that comes with it.

Your Amygdala Is Showing: Why Kids Get Heated Up

One of the great laughs on the playground when I was young came when one kid told another, "Your epidermis is showing!" The unsuspecting kid would usually check that his zipper was up, eliciting hysteria from everyone else, especially those who had already fallen for the prank and learned the hard way that "epidermis" just meant the outer layer of skin.

The amygdala, as mentioned earlier, is an almond-sized part of the brain chiefly responsible for strong emotions. Our amygdalae, while not visible the way our skin is, reveal their activity when we show strong emotions of anxiety, fear, or anger. In doing so, we're vulnerable to withdrawing and missing opportunities, to making impulsive decisions that are hardly decisions at all, and to being manipulated by others who see our weakened state. Being able to manage our amygdalae and the emotions they cause is a critical component in achieving success.

Generally, people who can manage these "hot" emotions are perceived to be calm and dependable. They may feel strong emotions at times, but they make use of the energy those emotions provide instead of being controlled by them. They also tend to be trusted. Whether you like the New England Patriots or not (and, I'm from New England, so need I say more?), Tom Brady is a master of staying calm under pressure.[42] It doesn't matter how far the team is behind and how little time is left on the clock, you know there is a chance to win if he is in the game.

⠿ Something to Try . . . to Show the Impact of Emotions on Thinking

First, try saying the word amygdala—it's a pretty cool word and a great conversation starter at parties. "Uh-mig-duh-la," with emphasis on the second syllable. Now, teach your child about the amygdala. One of the best ways is to use a visual made popular by Drs. Daniel Siegel and Tina Payne-Bryson.[43] Have your child make a fist but with the thumb inside. The thumb represents the amygdala while the front of the fingers represent the prefrontal cortex where Executive Function skills are generally managed. Point out that when someone is very upset and "flips his lid,"[44] it's as if the fingers jump up and

---

[42] For those in North Korea reading this, he is the quarterback of the best American football team in history.

[43] Siegel and Payne-Bryson, *The Whole-Brain Child*.

[44] Ibid.

expose his amygdala, leaving it in charge. When this happens, a person cannot think rationally at all. You may as well try breathing underwater. In fact, the equipment that is used to allow S.C.U.B.A. divers to breathe underwater is called a regulator. Pretty cool, isn't it? So, to allow our kids to manage stressful environments, they need to learn how to breathe, which regulates their emotional state.

Ask your child what, if anything, makes them go past being worried or frustrated to the point of being overwhelmed and feeling out of control. Ask your child what allows them to calm down again and feel better. Some of it is letting time pass, for some people it's a hug (and it's definitely not the case for others), sometimes it's a distraction, and, for many, it's sitting quietly and focusing on the breath. Start a list of reliable supports.

Consider the questions for yourself, as well. What sends you over that emotional cliff, and what does it take for you to return to and remain in a calm enough state that you feel capable of making good decisions again? Whether you have a leadership role in a company, in a family, or in the government, the ability to remain calm and retain one's composure is absolutely essential for making good decisions and for preventing ones that can have devastating effects.

Parents Are Not Cool: How Parents Raise the Heat

As someone who was definitely not born cool, I'll share my very simple secret to becoming slightly less uncool: thirty years of meditation, some therapy, regular exercise, sufficient sleep, and studying and teaching the issues raised in this book for decades. That's it! In other words, while getting better at managing emotions can be done, it's not just a matter of willpower in the moment. It's a lot of work over an extended period of time with successes and failures along the way.

From the get-go, being a parent is the ultimate test of our ability to stay cool. Our adorable infants deprive us of sleep, which is an essential factor in our self-regulation. Our stubborn toddlers can make us feel ridiculous; how can a tiny toddler say "no" so often and actually mean it? How is it that we can only get our way with them through primitive means, such as bribery or outright force? And, of course, we have our adolescents, who can make us feel outgunned in arguments by their teenage logic. Although their thinking may not make sense to us, somehow we can't seem to counter it. Then, when we adults raise our voices or say things that are regrettable (just once in a very rare while, hopefully), we feel frustrated with ourselves for our reactions, since we were supposed to be the adults. Maybe we blame our kids for provoking us; maybe we blame our parents for not being better models. Perhaps we take responsibility for our actions. I say, blame the amygdala . . . and then figure out how to do better next time.

Because we have the ability to think about the future in a way that other species don't, we also carry a certain angst that other species don't seem to. While that foresight can be an advantage, the worry and sometimes obsession it can provoke can cause us to become irrational and to express concerns with an anxiety that can hurt our children's confidence.[45] As our children mature, that protective instinct is not only less necessary but can become an impediment to their growth if we are too anxious to let them make mistakes. Of course, we have our concerns—"What if our kids are too rebellious, too inattentive, too lazy, too disobedient, too this or too that? Will they make it in the real world?"—but when we express that anxiety to our kids over and over again, they begin to wonder whether we

---

[45] See Robert Sapolsky's *Why Zebras Don't Get Ulcers.*

trust them, respect them, or even value them. Their hurt feelings often result in increasingly negative behavior, which intensifies our worry, which leads to greater self-doubt on their part and more acting out. This negative cycle will continue to worsen if we as adults have not learned how to slow down our reactions and keep our own cool. Our children do not need to know every time we are feeling anxious about them.

I have also come to believe that we, as parents, have a naturally conflicted relationship with our children because we have twin goals that are somewhat in conflict. On the one hand, we want them to be independent; on the other, we want them to listen to us, darn it![46] The timing for us to execute that shift, from "Do what I say because I said it," to "You need to figure out what to do," varies by child with no single indicator of when to do it. Is it time to push for change and independence or time for them to accept limits and for us to provide comfort and support?

If we wanted a society where parents were calmer and less susceptible to emotional stresses, we would pay professionals to raise children, not use biological or adoptive parents. A number of dystopian books, from *The Giver* to *Brave New World*, relegate child-rearing to professionals who do not share the same anxieties about their kids that those of us who have raised our own children feel. I mention these strange worlds because we deserve a bit of credit for our efforts. Raising kids is not only one of the most important jobs in the world, it's also among the hardest. To be effective, then, in teaching our children how to manage their anxieties, we must be patient with ourselves as we learn how to manage our own worries.

---

[46] The single best description of this that I have seen is in Barbara Kingsolver's *High Tide in Tucson,* an essay called "Civil Disobedience at the Breakfast Table."

Something to Try . . . When You Need to Manage Your Own Anxiety

Begin by acknowledging your own level of anxiety outside the context of being a parent—just where you tend to be in general. Do little things make you lose sleep and get you spiraling into a panic, or are you generally fairly mellow? How about with your children? Are you more stressed about them than with other things or able to take things more in stride? What sets you off and makes you anxious and even angry?

Whether or not you, yourself, tend toward anxiety, ask yourself about each of your children. What sets them off . . . and how badly? Is it being late for a sports practice or starting science homework? As you come to see that there are fairly predictable triggers for all of us, solutions will begin to present themselves.

Finally, ask yourself whether or not you judge yourself for feeling anxious and/or frustrated. If so, try to distinguish between the feelings and your actions. Do you actually do anything regrettable or simply feel things that are uncomfortable? It's helpful to accept that we're going to feel anxious and frustrated at times. However, we don't have to actually say or do anything that will undermine our children's sense that they're going to turn out okay.

From Hard to Impossible: The Nature of Vicious Cycles

Imagine that you are horrible at art. Or don't. You can just read about me in art class as a first grader, trying to draw my family and our home, just like every kid in the class. The teacher sees it, and I look up to see her reaction.

She is scowling, hesitating. "Michael, are you trying to be funny?"

I don't know what she means, so I shrug out of confusion. For some reason that I can't identify, I suddenly feel strange, like I don't belong in the room. A couple of kids nearby look over.

"Michael, I know you can do better than this. You're a smart kid. Stop trying to make the other kids laugh, and just do the best you can!"

I am trying, but I realize, suddenly, that my work is so bad that she can't believe it. Worse, she is unhappy with me. I feel dumb and mad at myself and don't want to draw anymore.

My anxiety around art probably began with that bad moment with that teacher, but it was the vicious cycle that I got into afterward that made me quit. Instead of giving me specific feedback or a pointer or two, my teacher doubted my intentions and pointed out my lack of natural talent in front of my peers. I felt embarrassed, and, over time, I consciously decided that I would not make an effort. I was so bad at art that I would rather make people laugh at my intentional goofs than try to succeed. As I got older, I played Pictionary not to win but to amuse. My drawings were sometimes legendary as friends would take them home, put them on their fridges, and ask people to guess what they were.

"Look what Michael drew. No, it's not a dog! No, it's not a deer! No, he was trying to draw a mailbox!"

Perhaps surprisingly, I actually did want to learn how to draw, but I was not going to keep trying when it only resulted in failure and humiliation. This is the vicious cycle depicted in figure 8a. When we don't do well at something, we can lose confidence, decide it's not worth the effort, and then, when we continue to do badly, confirm our belief that we simply can't do better. We can stay stuck in these vicious cycles for a very long time, whether it's for art, math, English, or being in relationships.

It took many years before I was willing to reconsider my conclusion that I would never be good at drawing. I was teaching and in my late twenties when a new art teacher joined our faculty. We became friends in spite of his love of art. Eventually, I told him my story, and he said that he would assume that I had plenty of potential. I was very observant and persistent, and I could apply those skills to drawing—if I wanted to, that is. And if I did want to, he could show me a less stressful way to approach art. He was so patient and had such a good approach that, reluctant as I was, I let him teach me some principles of drawing. I learned about aspects of art that I'd never heard of before, such as "value" (shading, basically), and I also learned about lowering my standards and not judging my progress so harshly. I saw, fairly quickly, that I could do much better than I'd imagined and started to gain confidence. A year later, on my honeymoon, I took a sketch journal with me and drew local landscapes and even birds. They're not too bad! I would even consider taking an art class when I retire.

It's amazing how we can have a dramatic shift in our orientation toward something. A caring friend, parent, or mentor can help us break out of our ruts and give us a chance to have enough success to want to go a little further. I was fortunate to have someone get me out of that cycle. He thought that all I really needed were a few skills and a chance to see my capabilities.

As explained in the Collaborative Problem Solving method originally developed by Drs. Ross Greene and Stuart Ablon, "These challenges are best understood as the byproduct of lagging thinking skills (rather than, for example, as attention-seeking, manipulative, limit-testing, or a sign of poor motivation); and second, that these challenges are best addressed by teaching children the skills they lack (rather than through reward and punishment programs and intensive imposition of adult will)."[47] In other words, if we want to help children escape this cycle, we can't just tell them to stop the nonsense; we need to teach them the skills they need to exit the cycle.

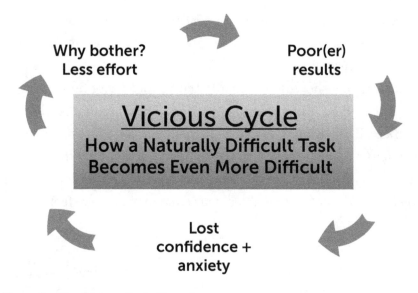

Figure 8a: The Vicious Cycle Overview

☀ Something to Try . . . When Your Child Is Caught in a Vicious Cycle

Identify some skill you tried to acquire or task you tried to complete and gave up on. Is it math? Cooking? Exercising? Playing an instrument? How much of your giving up is because the task or challenge is not at all interesting, and how much is because you got stuck at some point in the vicious cycle of failure and self-doubt?

---

[47] From http://www.thinkkids.org/learn/our-collaborative-problem-solving-approach/ See also Dr. Greene's newer work at https://www.cpsconnection.com/.

How about for your child? Has your child given up on something because it was difficult, and they lost confidence? Can you practically see the anxiety having led to this feeling of hopelessness? Try to resist the urge to tell your child how much confidence you have in them and that you know they can do it. Sometimes this can be taken as a not-so-subtle hint that they should be trying harder. Worse, it can be seen as being insincere.

Instead, try showing your child the Vicious Cycle figure and, if they are willing, fill one in together for something that is difficult for them. If you think it would be helpful, you can share one of your own first. See the example in figure 8b. What you may find is that the anxiety itself is making it more difficult to find solutions. When you look at the pattern together, your child may begin to feel calmer

Why bother?
Less effort
Example: I don't
practice piano

Poor(er)
results
Example: I can't get
through a tough
piano exercise

Vicious Cycle
How a Naturally Difficult Task
Becomes Even More Difficult

Lost
confidence +
anxiety
Example: I want to quit
piano because I'm
no good at it

Figure 8b: Example of The Vicious Cycle

about the situation and be able to generate solutions. I have witnessed numerous occasions where students learn about the Vicious Cycle and have epiphanies about why they have given up on something. It can be incredibly valuable in helping our children feel motivated to make a change.

A Not-So-Trivial Pursuit: The Front of the Hand Antidote

Todd was sitting glumly on his porch on the summer afternoon of our first meeting. He had failed two classes and had been placed on academic probation at his elite private school. In spite of being an outstanding athlete who was cool on the court, he tightened up on academic tests, not only while taking the tests but even while preparing for them. If he didn't figure out a solution soon, he would be forced to leave the school that he really liked, which made him even more nervous. You can see the Vicious Cycle that was beginning to unfold: failure, drop in confidence, giving up, more failure, more anxiety, and so forth. I noticed that he had the game Trivial Pursuit nearby and decided to try an experiment with him.

I picked a random card and asked him how much, on a scale of one to five, it would stress him to have to answer one of the questions without even knowing what the question was yet. He said it would be a four, very stressful, but he was willing to try. The question was, "Name the two biggest cities in Australia."

He said, "Well, I know Sydney is one of them, but I don't know *any* other cities in Australia, so I can't choose another city."

"None?" I asked. "If I were to list a few for you to choose among, what would your stress level be then?"

"Still a four," he said.

"Okay," I said. "Let's put this aside."

I showed him a pressure point on his hand that he could press and then asked him if he'd like to try the pressure point while I walked him through a progressive relaxation exercise. He agreed to try it and acknowledged that his stress level had moved to a two, almost no stress.

"So," I began, "while you press your hand, close your eyes and imagine your face relaxing, having no expression on it at all. Let your eyes relax, let your jaw relax—"

"Melbourne!" he yelled out.

"What?" I said.

"It's Melbourne," he said. "That's the other biggest city!"

What happened there? How did he suddenly acquire knowledge that he didn't even believe he had? While some would claim that he miraculously channeled it from a previous lifetime or that I had conveyed it to him through telepathy, it was clear that he had the information all along but couldn't access it when he was so anxious. Anxiety can make us forget almost anything, especially information that is not known very well in the first place. Conversely, being calm allows us access to our clearest, best thinking, allowing us to recall information we may not even know we had learned.

💡 Something to Try . . . When Kids Freeze Up During Tests

Teach your child the acronym HALT: Hungry, Anxious/Angry, Lonely, Tired. These obstacles are among those proven to demoralize us and to sap our motivation. When your child is deeply opposed to doing something, suggest that you both HALT and just consider if any of these four factors might be in play right now. If so, it's better to focus on taking care of those concerns before addressing whatever the problem was "supposed to" be.

You may also want to tell your child this story about Todd and Trivial Pursuit the next time your child is anxious about something coming up in school—not the analysis of it, just the story of a student who "didn't know" something and, once relaxed, suddenly did. Ask your child what they make of it. Is it possible that your child knows more than they think about something? If they have been spending a great deal of energy thinking and worrying about this challenge, perhaps doing something entirely different, such as playing Monopoly, shooting baskets, or going for a walk, will help unlock some of that knowledge. See if taking a break from the stress of non-stop focus allows your child to access the information more easily when they do return to study.

Pop Quiz: Knowing It "Like the Back of Your Hand" Antidote

Sometimes students tell me that they will do badly on a test, not because they don't know the material or because the test takes too long, but simply because they will "freak out," "go blank," or, in other words, suffer from crippling test anxiety. I understand where they are coming from because it's true for all of us if the conditions are wrong. What are those "wrong conditions" and how can we make them right?

A simple experiment can reveal a great deal. For many kids, the idea of an experiment can make them more nervous, so, although they're curious, they're not prepared to try it without further information. I tell them that it's a one-question pop quiz.

"I'm going to ask you your middle name in a moment," I say.

"Well, I can just tell you that," they say.

"Cool," I say, "but it's not that easy. I have to ask it *as a quiz*."

"What's the difference?" they ask.

"Well, you get nervous when you *know* it's a quiz, so in five seconds, I'm going to ask you your middle name, and you will only have ten seconds to provide the correct response. Okay, what is your middle name? Go," and I start counting to ten on my fingers.

Thus begins a productive, non-anxiety-producing conversation about just how well you have to know something in order to have no anxiety when being quizzed about it. Even in quiz conditions, having a quiz on what their middle name is, and knowing that this is what the quiz will be, does not provoke anxiety. We might go with slightly harder questions, such as "Name five colors," or "What is 7+3?" before moving toward the content of the actual quiz. The point, they realize, is that if they know it well enough, like the proverbial back of the hand, they really don't need to freak out. What is worrying them is either the content, or the directions, or the amount of time, or some other specific variable. That's it.

Try the "middle name quiz" with your child, exactly as described above. Most likely, your child will laugh. Help your child to notice how the anxiety level drops when they really know what they're doing.

Defeatist Perfectionists: The Lowered-Stakes Antidote

At an intake I was conducting, the puzzled parents told me that their daughter was very bright but had challenges starting her work. In meeting Hannah, a junior in high school, it was readily apparent that the problem was not getting started. Rather, the problem was attempting those steps where the teacher would evaluate the quality of her thinking.

In preparing to write a relatively straightforward five-page paper, one to be completed over the course of two weeks, this student had spent thirteen hours over the course of twelve days just to research the topic. With two days remaining, she hadn't written a single sentence of the paper. She had not drafted an outline. She hadn't even created a thesis statement, a central point that she would be arguing. Her parents had sensed that an implosion was imminent but were baffled as to why she would do this to herself.

Hannah was not afraid of hard work. She was afraid of being judged and, for that reason, couldn't bring herself to go from conducting research to making a claim. Her delay was primarily due to her anxiety. She spent all of her time focusing on what she knew she could do well, which was gathering more and more information. Doing so allowed her to avoid what she was uncertain about, which was taking a stance on the topic. As someone with a keen intellect, she was aware that more than one perspective would be defensible and was extremely worried about choosing the "wrong" one.

People who don't experience anxiety about being judged may be baffled by this "analysis paralysis." Most of us, though, can relate and have felt stymied by overthinking or stressing about something, whether it's a significant decision, such as which home to buy or what school to send our children to, or something small, such as what to order while the waitress is waiting for us. In cases like Hannah's, where the fear may not even be conscious and is severe enough to prevent the person from moving forward, a therapist may be the best solution. It depends, in large part, on what is the cause and what is the effect. Is incompetence on the task hurting our child's self-esteem, or is low self-esteem from other issues (biologically based depression, failures elsewhere, difficult life events) incapacitating our child on the task?

To see if the problem could be addressed by teaching Hannah a skill that might help her overcome her fear, I asked her to complete a sentence that began, "One thing I *might* be able to prove in this paper is that . . ." She looked at me.

"Might? What do you mean? Am I writing my thesis now?"

"Who knows? We can try a few of these," I said, "and one of them might stick. We're just throwing ideas out to see if anything might be useful later. The first few ideas usually aren't that good for most of us, so don't expect something brilliant from yourself yet. Brilliant comes later."

She offered, "Governments that concentrate power usually last longer than those that distribute it widely."

This proposal wasn't bad. While it was neither the most original thesis I'd ever seen nor the easiest to defend, it probably was good enough to earn her a decent grade. It certainly was interesting and arguable. She could either stick with it or change her mind about it after she assembled her main points. The important thing was that having this very rough "draft thesis" allowed her to have something to check her research against. In reviewing her extensive research, she would be able to refine her thesis, perhaps reversing it entirely or coming up with something brand new. Without a draft thesis, she would have remained stuck in neutral. Without a draft thesis, she could have and probably would have researched indefinitely, trying to do something to please the teacher while protecting herself from being judged. Without a draft thesis, she would have gotten no grade at all or failed because she never would have written the paper!

Choosing a side and risking being incorrect was the hard part for her. To avoid the possibility of being wrong, she continued to research, hoping to find the conclusive "right answer." Without that confidence, her anxiety was defeating her before she could even engage. That behavior is what gives rise to what I think of as "defeatist perfectionists," those who fail by never feeling they can do well enough. By giving Hannah some space to compose a draft thesis with the phrase "I might," she was able to tentatively commit to a point of view, knowing that she could modify it if necessary. She was surprised at how much easier it was to organize her thoughts and write the paper once she had taken an initial stand. Lowering the stakes can be the biggest factor in helping anxious kids get started. It allows them to focus on simply getting the work done and not get distracted by all of the things they could be doing to make it perfect.

Something to Try . . . When Your Child Fears Failure

If you know your child runs anxious or you suspect that is the case, instead of asking what is the best they can do or even what is something good they can do, ask for something that could be done for now "as an experiment to see if it's any good." You can add, "Beginnings usually aren't great, but, hey, that's where we have to start!"[48] These kinds of adages are difficult to argue with and allow your child to give in and trust you. Making the simple unproven assertion that "beginnings usually aren't great" shows empathy and allows them to consider your proposal to try an experiment.

Furthermore, by framing the experiment as something just to try out, there is far less pressure to get it right. Kids can be pretty headstrong when they're anxious, so it may require a few asks on your part before they'll try. You'll probably need the winning moves discussed in chapter 2 to find just the right timing and wording to get it right, but if they know you won't judge, you may be able to get them over the avoidance stage. It is worth mentioning that "overpraising" what

---

[48] "All beginnings are hard," says the character David Lurie in Chaim Potok's *In the Beginning*.

they produce will likely backfire. They are already hypercritical, and they won't be able to help themselves from feeling that everything is wrong if you focus on how great their work is. The best thing we can do is to acknowledge their effort and willingness to give it a shot. Saying "Hey, good for you for getting started. You can always make it better later if you have time, and you feel you need to," both compliments them sincerely and reassures them.

Blah, Blah, Blah: The Stopgap Antidote

Many people refer to writing as the greatest of Executive Function challenges,[49] and most of my students struggle to express themselves effectively in writing. For one of my students, an hour or even two of working on a handful of social studies questions led to the barest amount of information, perhaps four or five sentences to submit to the teacher. This student's parents compared it to him poking at his dinner, moving things around for a while but not actually eating anything. Perhaps, they surmised, it was his ADHD kicking in, that he was bored, so he couldn't focus. He wasn't bored.

What his parents didn't realize was that he had typed dozens of sentences and had then deleted them. The words he had written weren't quite the right ones, so he'd felt the need to start over. Sometimes, he couldn't come up with the right word and would stare at the screen for minutes at a time. Obviously, on a computer, all this wasted effort of doing and undoing wasn't even visible! All that his parents saw was a minimal amount of production, one that unfortunately did not match the considerable amount of effort he had invested. The student's perfectionism was perceived as a lack of focus and effort. He needed to be taught to get the work done more

---

[49] . . . but those people probably didn't raise children.

efficiently and not to belabor every word or even every sentence. It was an overnight homework assignment, not a dissertation, after all.

There's a saying among academicians, "Don't get it right. Get it written," and another by Supreme Court Justice Louis Brandeis, "There's no such thing as great writing, only great rewriting." This is a very difficult concept to convey to children because they want to do the right thing the first time. They don't want to have to deal with it later, and their default is to want our approval, or at least the teacher's, especially when they're young. It's our job to teach them the wisdom of these sayings, that "perfect is the enemy of the good," and so on.

The approach my students and I have taken is to actually write the words "BLAH BLAH BLAH" when they're stuck. It doesn't have to be all three "BLAHS," even one or two will do the trick, but it's got a nice ring to it. Kids love this technique because it's a bit weird, funny, and defiant. They can relax and just write down what does come easily and put in the BLAHS when they're stuck. No longer do they need to "get it write the first time."[50] Instead, they can get something down for now that is good enough and "fill in the 'blahs'" later, after they have gotten most of the heavy lifting out of the way and can see that the page is mostly filled in.

☀ Something to Try . . . When Dealing with Writer's Block

Try out the BLAH BLAH BLAH technique when your child has a paper to write or a lab to complete and is perseverating a bit (or a lot) on parts they cannot do at the moment. In fact, they're probably avoiding getting anything done and moving on because of these

---

[50] Pun and Billy Joel reference both intended.

worrisome aspects of the work. Have your child write the BLAHS in those blank spots and continue moving forward.

Another proven way to overcome inertia and to help your child start is to ask them to set five-minute goals. Rather than attempting to complete an entire assignment, have your child decide what they believe they can get done in just five minutes. First, they get to feel a sense of control over the situation by being allowed to name their focus. Second, by focusing on something very small and achievable, their anxiety diminishes. They don't have to climb the whole mountain right now.

I Do, We Do, You Do: The Toe-in-Water Antidote

People with Obsessive-Compulsive Disorder (OCD) can be hounded by some of the most extreme cases of anxiety, and some of the more promising non-medical treatments involve Cognitive Behavioral Therapy (CBT) and Exposure and Response Prevention (EX/RP).[51] A more generic use of these methods can benefit nearly everyone. With CBT, the big idea is to help people try small experiments, reflect on them, and change their beliefs and the messages they give themselves. With EX/RP, the essential idea is to be exposed to something stressful and to tolerate some distress while resisting the compulsion to act on obsessive and intrusive thoughts that arise. With both, the client benefits from the wisdom of a professional therapist who can guide them through their fears as they address their challenges.

While presenting to a group of professionals at one of the leading OCD clinics in the country, I demonstrated a tool for studying called the DKDK. It can be used for any student, even those students

---

51 National Institute of Mental Health, "Obsessive Compulsive Disorder."

who are too anxious to begin studying for a test. With this tool, the student sorts information, such as that found in their class notes or on a study guide, into three categories: things they know (K), things they don't know well enough yet (DK), and things they now realize they didn't even know that they didn't know (DKDK). That last category, the DKDK, may sound strange, but it simply refers to things they definitely do not know and may not even remember learning about, the things that they are surprised to be seeing as they start studying. This last section causes the greatest amount of anxiety.

Some students color-code the information by how well they know it, others put symbols such as check marks, X's, and exclamation marks, and still others write or type the information into three columns labeled with K, DK, and DKDK. The exercise proves remarkably helpful because it demonstrates to even the most anxious students that they do, in fact, know some of the material; and, for all students, it shows them where to prioritize. They begin with finding out what the DKDK parts even mean so that they are not mysterious and scary, and then tackle the DK so that weak sections get firmed up. When I taught this strategy to the professionals at the hospital, a senior psychologist raised her hand.

"What do you do for the kid who is so anxious that she won't even *look* at the study guide to *do* the DKDK? We have patients like that in this residential program."

That question was a great one. In those cases, the first thing we can do is empathize with them. Then, we can release them from the expectation that they will complete the exercise and, instead, offer to show them what to do. One general way to explain good teaching is "I do / we do / you do," which shifts responsibility gradually to the student. First, I model, then we work on assignments together, then they learn to do the work independently. For something intellectually tricky but not terribly anxiety provoking, the entire process may take twenty minutes. For challenges that evoke fear, the transfer of responsibility may take months and require a professional.

I explained that in this instance, my response would be, "I understand you don't want to do this and that it makes you very anxious. That's okay. I'm not going to force you to do it. Instead, I'll show you how I would approach it so that, someday, you will have this tool." I would say "someday" to remove any sense of urgency from the conversation. I have a strategy to show her that, if and when she's ready, she can adopt for herself. Then, I begin reviewing the notes and study guide and sharing my own thinking on the topic out loud.

"Okay, well, I don't know the Constitutional Convention, not well, anyway, so I'm going to mark that yellow. Then, there's this Connecticut Compromise. I have absolutely no idea on that one— that's a DKDK because I've never really heard of it, so that's a red for me."

When I do this in front of them, something interesting starts to happen. At some point, when they see me putting items in a "lower" column than would be true for them (saying DK for something that is K for them, or DKDK for something that is just DK for them), the student will jump in. It's just human nature. For example, I might say, "Thomas Jefferson . . . well, that's someone I've heard of, obviously, but I couldn't really tell you anything important about him."

The student will reply, "You know who he is!"

My response: "Well, duh. He helped write one of the important documents, and I think he served as president."

The student then says, "Obviously, but you know which document, right?"

I say, "I'm not sure I should guess. I'll probably get it wrong."

The student says, "It's the Declaration of Independence. And he practically wrote the whole thing! And he was the third president, for your information."

And everyone is a winner. Our kids have a chance to teach us or even correct us—their parents and teachers. What is more fun than that for them? At some point, the activity shifts from an "I do," in which they may or may not acknowledge me as I do the work, to a "we do" where we actively work together as a team, to, finally, a "you do," where I can shift to only offering help on an as-needed basis. With enough of these experiences, the child gains confidence, and the locus of control makes a slow but undeniable shift toward them leading the process.

Something to Try . . . When Your Child Is Frustrated

When your child is fed up with something or unwilling to start, and you sense that it's because they don't know how to do it, consider their anxiety. You can offer to think it through with them, but remember that that is a "we do." Are they ready for that yet? They may need you to lead with an "I do," in which case, try doing so in a way that allows them to correct you. Instead of breezing through or showing how smart you are at fifth grade math, or whatever it is, try focusing on the things you really don't know or would be happy to have your child correct you on.

Saying, "Help! Do you have any ideas on this one?" may lead your child to say, "Oh, Dad. Seriously? This isn't that bad."

Even if neither of you knows how to answer the question, it isn't a loss. You can research it on the internet, or make a note of it for your child to ask the teacher. You now have an excuse to ask your child to explain the work to you after he has met with the teacher. You're not judging that the work didn't get finished; it's just that you both took a crack at it and didn't solve it. Over time, your child will take a shot without you, and that's an even bigger win.

Don't Worry, Be Appy: The Electronic Antidote

A relatively easy way to help ourselves and our children when we are anxious is to use one of the increasing numbers of apps specifically designed to reduce stress and teach coping skills. Two that I have used with positive results are Calm.com and Headspace. Calm.com provides more immediate relief; it's kind of the Xanax of anti-stress apps. It's also a good "starter app," since it doesn't ask a great deal of you.

Headspace is a bigger investment in both time and cost; it also goes far deeper and aims for more lasting results. The mini-dharma talks—insight-oriented guidance in how to practice more effectively—are worth the price of admission. The result is more of a rewiring that builds calm and also insight for long-term change. It's more like exercise where, over time, benefits accumulate. Headspace also has an entire kids section now, with specific exercises designed for children based on their age and the issue being worked on. Another app worth noting is Insight Timer, a free app providing access for adults to a wide range of meditations.

You can also search the internet for free talks, videos, and relaxing music, as well as more apps of this type. Whether it's for stress or focus, these and other meditation and relaxation apps have a great deal of power and are becoming increasingly popular for good reason. Of course, like a gym membership, they must be used on a regular basis in order to be effective!

Something to Try . . . for Gaining Peace of Mind

Download an app for de-stressing. Try it yourself for ten days, every day, as early in the day as possible. Most of these apps will give you the first ten days for free. See how effective it is for you and whether it seems like it might be helpful for your child. Then, find a time when your child is receptive (knock before entering!) and tell them that you'd like them to try something and to give you feedback on it. This frame prevents it from either being a judgment of them ("You're such a mess; you really need this") or from being a directive from you. You'd like your child to try it and to tell you what they think. Whether or not they endorse it, you've at least shown a door to them. When they are ready, the help will be there for them.

Meditation for Math Tests: The Visualization Antidote

A lot of kids get anxious before math tests. Perhaps it's because the answers are either right or wrong most of the time; perhaps it's because the language of math is not our natural spoken language. Whatever the cause, test phobia seems particularly heightened for many students on math tests. For that reason, when I taught math classes, I made it a routine for students to have a moment of quiet calm before we started tests. They would put their heads down, and I would tell them to relax and just to notice their breathing and allow it to settle for a moment. I would remind them that they knew as much as they knew, and that they didn't need to impress me or their parents or even themselves, that all they needed to do now was to simply focus on the questions in front of them.

I reminded them of the basic test-taking techniques to use, such as writing down all of the formulas and notes they could remember right away, looking over all of the questions before starting, and skipping over questions that were too hard and returning later if they had time. The entire process only took about ninety seconds, but in their evaluations of the class, students consistently mentioned that taking the time to get centered was a huge part of why their math grades improved during the year. Managing this anxiety is such a valuable skill. Without that skill, it is particularly difficult to stay focused in those stressful situations.

> ### ☼ Something to Try . . . to Help Your Child Manage Math Anxiety

Since you're not going to be allowed into your child's classroom to lead them in a meditation—not only because the teacher won't let you, but your own kid probably wouldn't either!—you have four options.

1. Try to get your child's teacher to do something like what I have described. Some are very receptive to it and appreciate when parents support a more holistic and encouraging approach to learning, where testing is seen as part of the learning process and not as a means of calling out kids who haven't been working hard.
2. Lead your child in a meditation, visualization, or other form of relaxation yourself. Younger kids often love this.
3. Teach your child how to meditate so that she can do it for herself in any circumstance.
4. Get her support, either from an app, a coach, or a counselor who is knowledgeable. Bear in mind that the goal in any activity is for your child to become increasingly independent, so she can take the skills with her.

Summary: Keeping It Cool

Teaching our kids how to manage their anxiety and extricate themselves from the vicious cycles they can get stuck in is not an easy process. It requires us to be fairly "cool" ourselves. We do not need to embody the cool that emanates from Stephen Curry[52] or Beyoncé. We just need to be non-reactive and in command of our own emotional responses.

Our kids often have strong feelings. Our strong feelings, while understandable, will either distract from or escalate theirs. There is no scenario in which showing them how upset we are will help them to calm down and focus and do better. If we can keep calm and stay focused, we can help our children learn to adopt a similar posture. While it may be a "fake it 'til you make it" approach for us at the beginning, over time it will become more natural. Eventually, it will be our default.

When it comes to school, the other thing we can do is shift from telling them to do their "best" to telling them to do what makes sense for any given assignment. None of us have the time or the inclination to do our best on everything. We need to be choosy and to invest effort that is proportional to the importance of the task. We clean our homes every day to be sure, but we go to a different level when friends come over, and still another level when we are hosting a party with people we don't know as well. Kids need to be taught these kinds of distinctions to make similar judgments in their academic work.

Finally, even for very important tasks, perfect is, indeed, the enemy of good. If we want our children to have a modicum of sanity in their lives, then we need to teach them that even the most important things only require our "current best," not an absolute measure of perfection. There is a limited set of activities that require

---

[52] When fined $50,000 for the worst behavior of his career, throwing his mouthpiece toward a ref for a call he didn't like, Curry said, "[The issue was] losing my cool . . . I've got to be better than that." Haynes, "Curry Calls $50K Fine," *ESPN*.

perfection—testing the safety of a nuclear power plant or a space launch, for example—and even those things, while having a number of redundancies built in for protection, still have failures. Children do not benefit from feeling as though the challenges they face, in school or beyond, are at *that* level of urgency and criticality. They deserve the chance to make mistakes. They need to have a healthy degree of concern and motivation without being fearful. While too little push may encourage complacency, and too much may induce a feeling of hopelessness, the right amount of concern can help motivate a child to do his or her best.

Chapter 4

Focus in the Age of Attention: Directing the Distracted Child

Amateurs sit and wait for inspiration.
The rest of us just get up and go to work.

—Stephen King

Introduction: The Age of Attention

Nowadays, with smartphones and Google at our fingertips, information is a cheap commodity. In this era, the Age of Attention, people who can avoid distractions, dedicate their time to priorities, and concentrate for long periods of time come out on top. While the diagnosis of ADHD has spurred plenty of debate—what percentage of those diagnosed benefit substantially from medication, could schools do more to accommodate different types of learners to reduce the need for medication, and so forth—it is undisputed that attention is a valued resource and easily compromised in the modern world, where we often spend more time interacting with screens than with the people around us. According to a study of 2,600 children carried out by the nonprofit group Common Sense Media, eight-to-twelve-year-olds are using screen-based media for six hours a day on average while teenagers are using it for nine hours a day.[53] Obviously, somebody is not entirely focused when they are supposedly doing their homework!

With advertisers and acquaintances competing for our attention almost constantly, how can we stay focused? With our kids drawn toward the quicksand of social media and video games, how can we help them to slow down and to manage their impulsivity? How can we help them learn to focus long enough to get difficult things done? Attention is a multifaceted construct that includes the ability to resist impulses, to start tasks, to stay focused, and to finish a job, all while keeping the right amount of attention on competing priorities. This chapter provides direction to help your child learn how to get started (the skill of task initiation), and stay focused (the skill of sustained attention). Being able to direct their attention allows our children to do better on the more complex Executive Function skills discussed in chapters 5 and 6, such as how to organize, plan, and learn from experience.

Clueless: How to Upset the Teacher Without Really Trying

So this obnoxious teenager walks into the classroom. And he's sitting there whispering to his friend as the teacher tries to lead the class in what anyone would agree is a very good lesson being taught by a true pro. And the teacher is trying to hint ever-so-nicely to the student, with various looks, and gestures, and the clearing of his throat, and so on, that this student, who seems to think that his

---

[53] Wallace, "Teens Spend a 'Mind-Boggling' 9 Hours."

conversation is more important than anything the teacher is offering, needs to make better choices and focus on the issue at hand. But the kid goes on until finally there is no choice, really, but to say something directly to the student, even though it will interrupt the flow of the excellent lesson.

So the teacher looks at the student and says, "Mr. Delman, am I interrupting your conversation with your friend?"

And I look up at the teacher and say, "Yeah, but I'm gonna let it go this time."

And then the teacher, who is known for having an amazing sense of humor, does *not* give me a high five for cleverness or even laugh. He does not move on. He looks surprised and maybe hurt, as if I have betrayed him, and he sends me to the principal's office, a place I have been before but not since middle school. Question: What went wrong?

Well, some of my wise-guy response was simply me trying to show off for a laugh, but my rude behavior also had to do with my attention difficulties. Initially, I was distracted by the opportunity to talk to a friend. Then, I ignored the various cues to get back on track; I observed them, but I didn't feel the sense of urgency needed to tune in to the teacher. It wasn't just that I chose to ignore him. It was that my friend whispering to me seemed louder than the teacher speaking at full volume to the class. The teacher was talking generally; my friend was whispering specifically to me. That made a difference in what got my attention. When the teacher did address me directly, he definitely got my attention, but I wasn't thinking about the appropriate context. I replied impulsively with the first idea that popped into my head.

As understanding as I am of kids who cross the line as I did that day, I am well aware of the fact that the detention I received was a fair response. What was helpful was this teacher meeting with me to ask what I thought would be a good solution. I decided not to sit near my friend anymore, something I have a feeling would have been the result even if I hadn't come to that conclusion on my own. This teacher was masterful and allowed me to grow from the experience instead of relying only on his power to punish me. I'm sure he is one of the reasons why I went on to become an educator.

Kids with impulse control and attention challenges, some of the most fundamental of Executive Function skills, will need to develop tricks, tools, strategies, and discipline. Even those who take medication still need the skills just as those who wear glasses still need to learn how to read. Some of those skills, such as the PANTS technique in the next section, and specific note-taking strategies, such as those covered later in this chapter (see "Pushing Boundaries: How to Focus through Challenge"), are preventative. Doing them removes temptations so that our children can focus. Others, such as learning to apologize and to reflect on and change what is not working (see chapter 6), are used as a learning experience after a problem has occurred.

It is worth bearing in mind that there are some upsides to having challenges with impulsivity and/or attention if your child learns to master them. In education and in science, in business and in politics, there is a growing interest in neurodiversity, an approach to our brain differences that finds the pros and cons of various learning profiles so that we can all capitalize on our strengths and manage our weaknesses. People with ADHD, or who have a profile like someone with ADHD, often have great creativity and make novel connections.[54] Many possess a certain charisma that can allow them to motivate others. They can have energy to persist on hard work that can astonish others . . . as long as they're not bored. They can also develop

---

[54] While this claim of the benefits of neurodiversity are both overstated by some and rejected entirely by others, I have found an element of truth. See Thomas Armstrong's *Neurodiversity in the Classroom*.

empathy for others who struggle. For myself, diagnosis or not, the challenges and benefits of this sort of fidgety energy have led me to want to help kids do better, something I certainly did not imagine doing when I was a little whippersnapper mouthing off to teachers I adored. Maybe it's karma.

Get Your Pants On: How to Focus in Class

Kids today are criticized for so many things, many of which are not entirely fair. If they made an effort to have their pants on in class, I would predict that many teachers would have a better opinion of them. By pants, I am referring to an acronym for Posture, Asking questions, Note-taking, Tracking the speaker, and Smiling (PANTS). It's remarkable how beneficial some relatively superficial changes can be. When students practice these five behaviors in class, three things happen.

First, they themselves change. Sitting up straight, getting questions answered, taking notes, following the speaker with one's eyes, and occasionally smiling at the teacher—all of these things help a student to be more attentive. Being in the moment and staying alert capitalizes on whatever capacities we have and boosts our interest in the material. It makes students more likely to make connections between what is going on in the classroom and what matters to them outside of the classroom. It also builds the habit of staying attentive.

Second, when students demonstrate that they are attentive, the teachers think better of them. Teachers really appreciate it when students show that they care about the lesson and find the teacher to be offering something of value. While some teachers may be sympathetic to students who appear to be disengaged, many will not. Many teachers lack either the patience or the insight to feel committed to a student who is slouching and looks unhappy to be in class. In fact, teachers are likely to feel somewhat insulted by and, therefore, not sympathetic toward a student who appears to be bored by the subject the teacher is passionate about. Consciously or not, teachers will go out of their way to support students who are asking thoughtful questions and paying attention. The teacher will smile back at the student who smiles at them, perhaps get to know the student as an individual, and ask questions about their extracurricular activities. The teacher will offer tips on how to succeed in their class, and it's possible that a close grade will go the student's way because of a "good attitude."

All of this leads to the third benefit, which is the student's self-perception. Students getting this kind of positive feedback and support from teachers start to believe in themselves more. They recognize that an authority figure likes them and, over time, may come to believe that the teacher thinks they're smart. While few kids really want to be the teacher's pet, most young people feel good about being valued by someone in a position of power. As they receive the benefits of being appreciated by the teachers, they tend to become more receptive to doing things even more effectively and to working harder. It starts the Cycle of Growth (figure 10).

While most kids will learn these skills over time, it can be a painful learning process with some significant costs along the way if your child is zero out of five on the PANTS score. If your child is young and open to your help, you can be the one to teach the skills. If your child is older, usually sixth grade or beyond, it's better to assign the task to a cool aunt, uncle, or friend, or to have someone at school help out. For those kids who really struggle as they enter middle school or even earlier, perhaps because they have a social skills disorder, Asperger's or other diagnosis on the autism spectrum, or very significant and untreated ADHD, learning the skills may require a professional. In those cases, you might consider seeing your school's counselor for support.

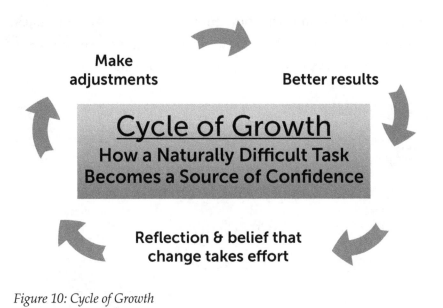

Figure 10: Cycle of Growth

Something to Try . . . to Develop the Skill of Engagement

Have a family meal and commit to everyone practicing good posture, looking at the person speaking, asking a question of the speaker, and trying to find occasion to smile. Taking notes? That would be funny at the dinner table and is not recommended.

For note-taking, try enlisting your child in a "cool chore," one where they feel really engaged because the chore itself is interesting or there's a relevant reward that naturally comes from it. For example, have them write down the ingredients for a recipe that you'll be shopping for and cooking. Obviously, the recipe needs to be for something your child likes to eat or at least to prepare. Another example would be to have your youngest take notes while the family brainstorms ideas of where to go for a fun day out or for a dinner at a restaurant. You can teach your child how to organize their notes by having a space for each option and drawing lines off each option with reasons attached to the options. See figure 11.

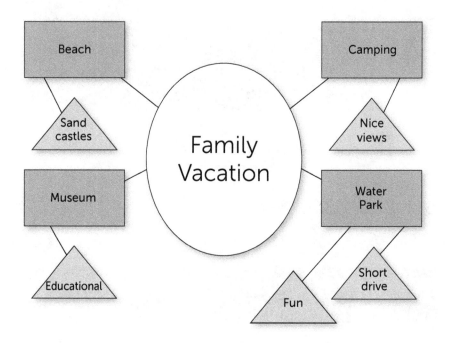

Figure 11: Note-Taking Graphic Organizer

For any note-taking activity, return to the topic several days later, so your child sees the value of having notes. Ask a question, such as, "What were the reasons we came up with for choosing the water park?" Showing your child a week later that their diagram and notes were useful in making a decision proves that you take your child seriously. That's money in the bank for your relationship and a confidence booster for your child. It's also developing that particular skill and orientation for the classroom.

Wait, Wait—Too Late: How to Up the Urgency

To nobody's surprise, my student Nate didn't do his reading and, consequently, failed his English quiz. He told me that he wanted to do better next time, and before I could say, "Work harder and smarter," he acknowledged that he needed to plan more effectively.

"So, what actually happens? How does the reading problem play out?" I asked.

"I don't start the reading until the night before," he said.

"And then you run out of time trying to do it all in one night?" I guessed.

"No, it's worse than that," he said. "By the time I've decided I have to do it, I'm actually too anxious to do it."

It seemed like two somewhat separate problems—the waiting in the first place, and then the being unable to do it because he was overwhelmed. I asked him if he knew why he waited.

"Sure. I wait because it doesn't take very long. They give us a week to do it, and I don't need a week," he said, as if it were the most reasonable thing in the world.

If I were one of his parents, I am pretty sure I would have said something like, "So you wait until the night before and then don't do it all? Where's the sense in that? Answer, pal: There is none!"

Thankfully, I was wearing my professional hat. I simply said, "Got it. Let's do the math to figure out how long you'll need." (He loves math.) "How much total time do you need and over how many days?"

He estimated that he would need about four hours for the fifteen chapters, and that he could do it all in one night. I asked if he had ever done that successfully before. He hedged a bit. "I have done it in one night. The quiz grade wasn't good, but that was because I didn't know what the format of the test would be."

Knowing that he might not be ready to make a change and overcome his panic-inducing delays, I asked whether he really wanted to plan out his work over the course of the week or if he just wanted to learn how to cram more effectively. While I am an Executive Function coach and obviously not trying to encourage a lifetime of bad habits, I understood that he was already taking a step forward just to have this conversation with me. It was a shift into Contemplation after years of being in denial. I could keep helping him advance, but it would have to be more or less at his pace.

"Honestly? I'd rather just do it the night before," he replied. Well, it was honest at least.

I asked what it was like for him when he tried to start as soon as an assignment was given. He said that he felt no energy and lost focus quickly. I explained that the lack of energy and motivation he experienced was true for almost everyone, but especially for those with ADHD. There is a peak performance curve (see figure 12) that illustrates how we need the right amount of challenge to be both calm and energized and, thereby, to do our best. If Nate tried to start too early, he would have too little motivation and insufficient energy. As the deadline approached, he gained energy through a healthy amount of anxiety. If he waited too long, however, he wouldn't be able to overcome that anxiety.

The question I asked him then was, "What is the 'just right level of anxiety' for you? When do you have just enough energy to want to start and not so much anxiety that you can't start?

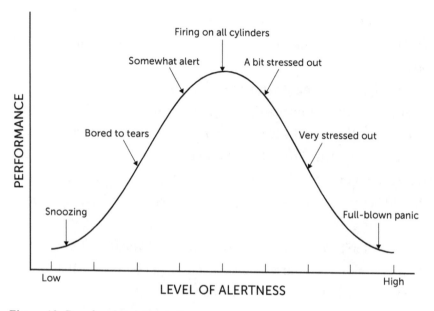

Figure 12: Boredom/anxiety continuum

Given his love of math and science, I compared it to the calculations needed to pull the United States' first spacecrafts out of orbit and back to Earth by shifting from an elliptical to a parabolic arc. True, I didn't really know what I was saying (seeing the movie *Hidden Figures* didn't exactly make me an expert), but he appreciated my effort and got the point. Too early or too late = not good. We need just the right timing to get out of the orbit and achieve a landing.

"What message goes through your head when you have enough motivation to do the work, but you're not yet freaked out about it?" I continued.

"I start thinking, 'I need to do this now.' But if I wait too long, I start thinking, 'I should have done this already.'"

"When does that 'I need to do this now' message pop up?"

"Usually, with two to three days to go."

"You sure? Not just on the last day?" I asked, to underscore the point for him.

"No, I start feeling it with a few days to go."

Again, I almost jumped to say, "Why don't you listen to that voice?" but that would have been a crucial mistake. Since he was already ambivalent, I didn't want him becoming defensive and coming up with every possible reason to delay.[55] Instead, I cut myself off mid-sentence and asked a question designed to have him focus on changing.

"Why don't you . . . celebrate for a moment? You're definitely hearing the 'time-to-get-started voice.' Now, what would be the upside of getting started once you hear that voice?"

"I'd have a lot less hanging over me the last night!" he said. "Also, I'd definitely do a better job. Plus, my parents wouldn't be bothering me about it."

Suddenly, he was articulating the reasons why he would be better off with better planning and time management skills.

"So, do you actually hear that voice seven days ahead?" I asked.

"Well, yeah, from my mom."

"What about from yourself?"

"No, not yet. Like I said, I hear a 'get going' message two to three days before it's due."

"And why do you hear it then?"

"Because that's how long I need."

Now was the right time to ask him why he chose to delay.

---

55 For more on how to use this kind of "change talk," conversations that evoke change instead of maintaining the status quo, see Arkowitz, Miller, and Rollnick, *Motivational Interviewing in the Treatment of Psychological Problems*.

"Well, it's kind of funny. I had already told my parents that I finished the work because that's what they were expecting, so I would have to hide from them that I was doing the reading now or admit I'd been lying before."

How ironic that he would have to hide getting his work done from his parents in order to let them keep believing the lie. The result was not doing the work. The bottom line turned out to be three simple solutions:

- Identify how long he really needed and when to start

- Parents stay out

- Start on time, neither early nor late

My using a bit of inquiry allowed him to discover for himself how he could solve his own problem. He had found a way to get himself moving, and it really boiled down to listening to his own voice telling him when he needed to start.

Something to Try . . . When Your Child Needs Help Starting Work at the Right Time

Try to figure out your child's peak performance timeline. Do they run very anxious and need to start things early? Even then, do you need to find ways to calm them down so they can start at all? If so, two things really help: having specific methods of letting go of emotional stress, and breaking things down into smaller pieces to focus on. These planning methods are explained in the following chapter on higher-level Executive Function skills. (See "Planning . . . to Get

It Done: Basic Project Management Skills.") For now, simply identify the fact that anxiety is preventing your child from even beginning.

If, on the other hand, your child is not getting started because they do not estimate time very well, don't have much investment in the assignment, or are overconfident, then your goal is to inject a sense of urgency into the situation. For kids like this, we need to demonstrate the relevance of the work, shorten the time frame, and transform what is boring into a challenge or a game. (See, for example, "Making a Bet: How to Get a Kid to Review Work" at the end of this chapter.)

The Fast Break: How to End Homework Battles

While a number of adults have jobs that require us to work extremely long hours and bring our work home or to work two or more jobs, it is unreasonable, in my opinion, to require that level of continuous work from children. While I can justify a modest amount of homework assigned with clear goals explained to the students and parents, I still would expect most children to feel some resentment about it. They have already been to work all day at a job they had no say in choosing (that would be school), and where they are often forced to demonstrate their skills or incompetence in front of their peers. Now, they have to do more work at home with even less support than at school while being told by their other bosses (that would be us parents) how important it is that they do their very best. It's a wonder more kids don't rebel or give up when we consider how much we ask of them in this regard.

We still want and expect our children to do the work, but we can understand if they're not excited to dive right in the moment they return from school. Often, our kids avoid the work by telling us they don't have much to do and will do it "later," which does not reassure us a great deal. Perhaps they will start it, but it will be so late at night that it will be done badly, or they will be exhausted the next day.

One of the greatest solutions for getting them to start homework at a reasonable time is to allow them to delay the official start time with a tool my company developed called the "Fast Break." With this approach, students take a "Fast Break" when they get home from school, and then draft a plan for their homework rather than necessarily begin the work itself. The plan has three critical features with an option to upgrade at no extra charge. The first feature is that they list the amount of time they think they will need for each assignment, which is valuable for two reasons. Estimating time shows kids for themselves what kind of night it's going to be if they are to do a good job. That estimate allows them to plan their time well. In addition, students ultimately get better at making accurate estimates and learn whether they chronically over- or underestimate how long things will take.

The second feature of the Fast Break is sequencing the homework in a logical way. While some students need to start with something on the easier side to build some momentum, tackling the toughest material earlier in the afternoon is generally a good idea. Starting the most dreaded assignment when already fatigued at the end of the night is a self-fulfilling prophecy for failure.

The third feature is to dedicate a specific time for each activity. There are several ways to do this, such as putting the tasks in chronological order on a spreadsheet (see figure 13a) or simply noting it by hand on a piece of paper. Allocating specific time for breaks also helps. It's nice for a student to know that something pleasant will follow some hard work, and it's important for them to know when the next task must be started.

3:00–3:30	*Chill out, eat snack*
3:30–4:15	**History reading and ?s**
4:15–4:20	*Read sports online*
4:20–4:55	**Science facts on Quizlet**
5:00–6:00	**Finish HW and read**
6:00–7:00	*Dinner, chat online with friends*
7:00–8:00	**Read book**
8:00 ⇢	*Done! Watch sports on TV*

Figure 13a: Fast Break, Basic Version

Using the Fast Break or something similar[56] allows your child to know where they stand for the remainder of the day and to stay focused on just one thing at a time when they are working. Instead of worrying about all of the assignments all of the time or avoiding

		ELA	Geometry	European History	Earth Science	Commitment	Total
1/30	Tues	Read ch. 2, 30, 8-8:30	Prep quiz, DKDK, 15, 7:45	Text pages and define terms, 30, free block	Lab questions, 30, 9-9:30	Ski team, 3-7	1:15 at home
1/31	Wed	Read ch. 3, 30, 8-8:30	See teacher X block, Quizlet for terms, 30 7:00	DKDK (30) and anticipate essay (30), 6-7	Lab graph, (20-30), waves questions (20) – during free	Ski team, 3-5	2 hours
2/1	Th	Read ch. 4, 30, 9-9:30	Practice problems, 30, 4:30-5	Thesis and bullets of 3 likely essays, 45, 5-6	Lab Due	Workout, 3-4	1:45
2/2	Fri	X	QUIZ (10 pts)	QUIZ (25-30 pts)	X	Sleepover	none
2/3	Sat	X	X	Brainstorm / research, 30, ?	X		30
2/4	Sun	Read ch. 5, 30	X	Outline in-class paper, 1 hour, 7-8	X	Family Game Night	1:30
2/5	Mon	?	?	SHORT PAPER (25-30 pts)			

Figure 13b: Fast Break, Expanded Version

---

[56] An app called 30/30 provides a similar structure, showing when all tasks will be completed and counting down the time remaining. Thank you to Sarah Ward of Cognitive Connections for pointing this one out to me.

them, your child has created a time for each thing so that each thing can be done on time. For older students, the version in figure 13b shows a way to manage all subjects over longer stretches of time.

If your child doesn't happen to be a huge homework fan (it's possible), try telling them that you have learned about a tool that will let them get a good idea of what they'll need to do and when so that they can have some breaks and concentrated free time tonight. If they're anxious, let them know that it tends to help people relax as well as focus, since this method shows when they will do each task. Once your child knows how to allocate work and stay focused on it for the prescribed amount of time, the Fast Break will be an easy and obvious tool to use. The benefits of getting work done more quickly and with less anxiety will be convincing enough. Your child might even get invested enough to make their own modifications that make it more useful for them.

Roll of the Dice: How to Avoid Needless Delays

Our children's attention is a precious commodity. It's helpful to remember this somewhat obvious but easily forgotten fact when we are discussing with them something that we find important or interesting but they do not. Sometimes, the best thing we can do to help them with schoolwork is to help them move on from relatively unimportant tasks to those that matter more. Whether it's "over-researching" due to anxiety (as in "Defeatist Perfectionists" from the previous chapter) or fiddling with the fonts out of boredom, procrastinating doing the hardest aspects of the work leads to running out of energy.

I worked with a student whose teacher had intended to be generous and flexible by allowing the students to choose among twenty different topics and five options for how to present them. That night, students had to decide which topic and which style of presentation they wanted, list three sources, and draft a thesis statement. My entire hour with this student could have been spent evaluating the various topics and presentation options to ensure that we had the perfect choice. Instead, I began by asking him which he preferred.

"That would be 'none of the above,'" he said. "And thank you for asking."

"Well, contestant #1, are there any you dislike more than the others?" I asked, my plan being to narrow the list first in order to speed up the process.

"No, Chuck," he said, continuing our game show approach. "They're all super boring."

After confirming that all choices were equally bad, I asked him to simply pick a number from one to twenty without looking, making it a roll of the dice, essentially. He did, and I asked him if he was okay with focusing on the number we landed on: The United Nations' Declaration of Human Rights as it pertained to environmental sustainability.

He smiled and said, "Sure, whatever."

I asked him if he would like to switch to another topic, and he again confirmed that he had no greater interest in any of the other topics. Then, I asked him about options for how he would do the presentation and received a very different answer and tone.

"Yeah," he said, "I'm going to write a poem that I could possibly turn into a song."

For him, the style mattered quite a bit, while he was indifferent to the subject matter, since all of it was relatively uninteresting to him. By selecting the topic and approach quickly, we were able to utilize the bulk of the hour gathering information and discussing how he would formulate a thesis statement once I left. For some students, spending time on choosing a topic that would sustain their interest would have been a good investment. For this student, the more helpful approach was to work efficiently toward completion of the assignment.

Scream-Worthy Screens: How to Tame the Beasts

Perhaps you can relate to my love/hate relationship with the phone. I love *my* phone (most of the time) but typically feel bent out of shape about my younger daughter's phone. It's not that I don't think it's worthwhile for her to spend six hours a day on Snapchat, another five hours on Instagram, and seventeen more hours on other phone-related activities. Actually, that is precisely it.

I don't think it's a good use of her time when that happens, and while I've spoken with enough substance abuse experts to not label her love of the phone an addiction, it's certainly a concern for me. I realize that part of the reason that I struggle with her connection to the phone is because I don't truly get it. I don't feel the need she does to be constantly connected to people. Some of it is my being older and not needing or even wanting the constant contact that teenagers want, and some of it is a generational gap. Her generation grew up as digital natives and think of their phones as a natural way to stay in touch whenever they want, whereas we had to take turns using the phone when growing up, and it sure didn't have the bells and whistles. We thought in terms of minutes per day; they use their devices for hours per day.

To be fair and put it in perspective, my daughter is a good kid who does well in school, plays sports whenever she can, has plenty of friends (sometimes part of the problem as well as a great thing), and is more than able to converse with all sorts of people in person without staring at the ground. And yet, and yet . . . I still feel that there have to be limits, perhaps for health reasons, certainly because there are other good things to do with her time, partly for the discipline of not overindulging too often. I want my kids to invest their time and focus their attention, for the most part, on things that are of value, and the phone activities often don't meet my snobby threshold. How many music videos or chat messages in a day are really worth her while?

I also am aware of my professional bias as an Executive Function coach. It's important to me that she learns to be aware of her time and not squander it. I have tried a number of tactics, including negotiating an amount of time that seemed reasonable to both of us, but she never kept track and my constantly checking in drove both of us slightly crazy. She was not aware of her usage of the phone and constantly ran over, never developing the time awareness I had wanted for her. Moreover, the constant back and forth put a strain on our relationship.

I then tried letting her decide for herself how much to use the phone, with two caveats. First, she had to track her usage twice a day, recording the total time and also her time on her two favorite apps, since they were taking almost 80 percent of the total. Second, the phone could never be used as an excuse for not doing more important activities. Her success at tracking, however, was negligible, and she never bought into this system that I imposed. She is not a rule follower and either needs to see the benefits herself of making a personal change or have consequences that mean something to her and seem reasonable. This entire experiment proved that the two of us needed a bit more support, possibly professional help!

We switched over to and are still using an app called ScreenTime, which has been a helpful solution for a small fee. After discussing the matter with her, I set a total daily phone limit for school days and another for weekends, and when she reaches that limit, the phone can only be used for basic communications (phone and text). She has developed the skill of self-monitoring and time management through this process, as she truly does not want to run out of the fun stuff before the end of the day.

The app also allows her to earn time back if she completes tasks we've mutually agreed upon. While I would love for her to want to manage her screen time well simply because she herself sees how important it is, she's not entirely there yet; and at this stage, I'm helping her to build better habits that improve some of her Executive Function skills. She is paying better attention to her use of time, knowing that she needs to value it. That type of awareness will serve her well in high school, college, and any work environment where sustained focus will be necessary to do well with limited time and higher demands.

Something to Try . . . When Screen Time Is a Problem

Phones are the cars of today. Everyone needs one to go anywhere and be a part of things. It is incumbent on us to figure out with our children the rules of the road on these devices. What time limits are useful? Why? We also need to determine how involved we want to be. Some apps will allow you to see all of your child's exact interactions on their social media. Do you want that level of detail, or do you want to set general expectations and give your child the benefit of the doubt on the actual use of the apps?

Expect this conversation to be several conversations, and be prepared to make revisions to your plans. The goal is not to punish but to enlighten and to develop self-discipline. One day your kid will be driving that baby without you.

Phones aren't the only screens we need to tame. Fortunately, there are plenty of ways to shut down or diminish access to distracting sites on laptops and desktops. As a Mac user, I like Self-Control, an app that allows you to blacklist sites you wish to avoid for a specified period of time while you focus on your work. Even the name itself supports the development of Executive Function skills, since it works best when students choose to use it themselves instead of having it imposed on them by their parents. There are plenty of alternatives, such as Freedom and Cold Turkey for Macs, Stay Focused for PCs, and FocusMe for both. I have had numerous students tell me that their focus and productivity have increased dramatically simply by using these types of apps on their various screens.

It is also worth mentioning f.lux and other light-altering apps, ones that, increasingly, are bundled into phones and other computers. As the daylight wanes, these apps shift screens from emitting stimulating blue light to a more relaxing red light, gently moving us toward a retreat from the screen and toward bed. This one is a game-changer, too, letting us remove our attention from something that is very difficult to leave. Check the settings in the Clock app for your phone and download the software for your laptop if it's not already built in.

Next Steps: How to Return from a Break

Once our kids have started on the work and perhaps attained a degree of momentum, we might worry about allowing them to take a break, knowing how difficult it can be to get them to return from it. While breaks, for us and our kids, have that element of risk, they are not optional. We all need them to maintain our energy and focus. Taking a few minutes to sit quietly, or thirty minutes to exercise, allows us to replenish our energy and attention. How can we maximize the odds that our children will come back in a timely way after a break or, indeed, come back at all that day? Better still, is there anything we can do to set the stage for them to return with some enthusiasm and not to give up after one burst of effort on their work?

The first general principle is to have our children take a break at the right time, *before* they are demoralized. Developing fortitude is great, but working when hungry, exhausted, or in desperate need of a bathroom break is poor thinking. Remember HALT—hungry, angry/anxious, lonely, tired—and encourage these healthy breaks. It actually takes a degree of discipline to remember to take appropriate breaks. Help your child schedule regular breaks, timing the work so that there is a reminder to pause, or determining a fixed place to stop for a break (after completing ten math problems, for example).

Second, they need to reduce the stress of coming back by having a plan of what they will do after they return. One of the great and simple methods for helping our children to take a needed break that simultaneously sets them up to return with a sense of purpose is to jot down what their next steps will be after the break. "After the break, I will _____." Whatever that thing is, they no longer need to worry that they'll forget to do it. It's on a "To-Do" list, or it's in the assignment book, or it's written right on the assignment itself. "Spice up vocabulary," or "double-check problems 7 and 12," is written down. They can then immerse themselves in a timed break without worry. Upon returning, they don't have to determine a plan. They have already done that for themselves ahead of time. They have momentum and can get right back into the work without having to cogitate, deliberate, or ruminate.

Try the "Next Steps" approach yourself before recommending it to your child. See if it does, in fact, give you a sense of confidence and allow you to take breaks with a greater sense of enjoyment. See if it makes you less reluctant to return to the task after the break. Then, try it with your child. See if this pre-planning helps them to sustain their effort for each sprint of work and if it facilitates a smoother transition back to the work following the break.

Pushing Boundaries: How to Focus through Challenge

For some students, their minds move quickly—so quickly that they have difficulty focusing in class. These students may have fast processing speed but poor impulse control.[57] Because of this combination, they are likely to feel restless in class, wanting to check on their thinking right away and to engage in a debate rather than sit passively taking notes and waiting their turn to speak just once in an hour-long class. That sitting time feels like prison time for them, and they'll keep themselves entertained by coming up with clever and often inappropriate comments. For these students, it's not that they can't keep up because they can't pay attention. It's that they can't pay attention because they are ahead of the class.

When I was a principal, one eighth grader was sent to my office several times for being rude to the teacher. At first, I tried the more typical approaches used with disruptive students—trying to get him to see the consequences for the other students, considering the impact on his own grade, letting him know that he would not be able to be in the classroom if he kept up his poor behavior—all to no avail. Seen in the context of him being bright but impulsive, I began to understand that he felt that he was the aggrieved party. He did not want to be in the classroom, which was designed well for most of the kids in the room but was dull for him. Challenging the teacher was his way of staying engaged. Making ridiculous jokes prevented him from feeling

---

[57] For students who struggle with slower processing speed, see *Bright Kids Who Can't Keep Up* by Drs. Ellen Braaten and Brian Willoughby.

frustrated about having to listen to information he already knew or could grasp more quickly than most of his classmates.

Although both educators and outsiders may have seen him as arrogant for resenting school and for judging the teacher and school as being inadequate, I agreed with him on a key point: He needed more challenge, and he needed it during class. With the cooperation of his teacher, we found a solution. During class, he was to write down questions that he thought the teacher wouldn't be able to answer, and after class, he would see if she could. This approach turned each class into an extended game with a reward at the end. "Stump the Teacher" became his goal, but whether he won or lost, he still won. If he stumped her, he got a point for his pride. If he didn't, she impressed him a bit more. Either way, he was hanging on her every word to look for something to challenge. In the end, they built a positive relationship because she was impressed that he was so invested, and he was impressed by her wide range of knowledge and ability to answer his questions. Initially, this student had believed that he was smarter than the teacher. Handicapped by having to move at the pace of the entire class, she would, of course, not be able to display her full range of knowledge. Having a one-on-one check-in/debate with him, however, freed her to pull out all the stops so they could have interesting exchanges. For very astute and easily bored students like Billy—students who can go to schools like MIT, as he did, and who love adrenaline (he's a pilot now, among other things)—it's critical to provide a challenge.

Something to Try . . . to Make Note-Taking Worthwhile

Another solution, especially for busy students or teachers who may not have the chance for such regular check-ins, is for the student to take notes in class as if they are preparing for the next test. Taking notes in an organized fashion allows students to stay engaged in class, preventing acting-out behavior and showing the teacher that they are invested in the learning. The biggest sell for these students, in many cases, is that they will have less studying to do at home. Since they'll be doing much of the thinking and organizing in the classroom, they will be steps ahead in the homework and for tests. They'll also find the classroom experience to be more meaningful. Less boredom and more free time? It's a pretty appealing offer.

If the teacher is providing a PowerPoint or other guided notes, your child can just fill in additional information and questions on the handouts. If the teacher hasn't provided anything, your child can create a semantic map. (See figure 13.) This method allows your child to see general areas of information. Third, your child can create a three-column recall (see figure 14) that turns easily into a

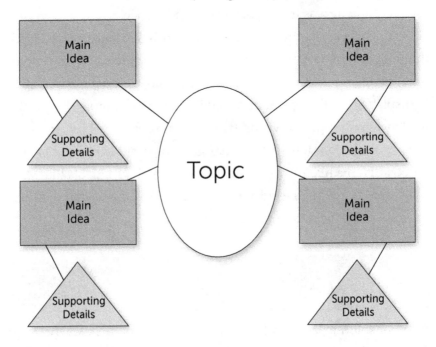

Figure 13: Semantic Map

study guide with a simple fold of the paper. The basic idea is to put key words or phrases in the first column, some elaboration in the second column, and reactions (such as comments, connections, and questions) in the third column. Finally, the Cornell notes system (see figure 15) is a traditional method for college note-taking that can certainly be used by high school students and even middle school students. It lets students focus on the lecture by capturing key ideas and associations to them; it also serves as a good study guide later. All of these methods keep students actively focused.

Key words/phrases	Details	Reactions
Example: Connecticut Compromise	1787 Bicameral legislature AKA Great Compromise Wins by narrow margin	Did small states get a better deal as a result?

Figure 14: Three-Column Recall

Key ideas	Details and connections
Example: Connecticut Compromise = big states and small states get wins	1787 Agreement @ Constitutional Convention Bicameral legislature AKA Great Compromise or Sherman Compromise Wins by 1 vote

Summary
Connecticut Compromise got the right balance so all states could agree on a method of bicameral legislation at the Constitutional Convention

Figure 15: Cornell Notes

Making a Bet: How to Get a Kid to Review Work

Asking most kids to review their work for errors or places to improve is like asking someone who just climbed a mountain to go back down and to do it again and stay on the trail a bit more perfectly. Okay, perhaps it's not, but it can feel like that. Listen to the tone of a child who says, "I'm done" on a homework assignment. Most of the time they're saying it definitively and not seeking opportunities to improve said work. That box has been checked off! For a kid with Executive Function challenges, especially those associated with ADHD such as impulse control or sustained attention, that feeling of being done is tough to override.

How can we get them to slow down a little and to invest a bit of time reviewing their work? How do we get them to pause and check that they have paid sufficient attention to all parts of the homework or to all parts of the studying for the test? How can we get them to focus on the importance of reviewing their work when they typically see it as unnecessary? Worse still, from their point of view, double-checking their work means missing time with friends on social media and gaming, to keep working on something that they didn't like doing in the first place!

One of my students was conjugating verbs to prepare for her French test and finished very quickly—a bit too quickly.

"Okay, got them!" she said.

"You sure?" I asked.

"Yep," she replied, without hesitating.

"How sure?" I followed up, having noticed at least one error.

"I'm sure, okay?" she said, indicating that we could now move on to other things.

"Are you ten dollars sure?" I asked.

She paused and then asked, "What do you mean?"

"If you're sure it's perfect, let's bet ten dollars. I'll pay you ten dollars if it's perfect, and if it's not, you pay me ten dollars."

She hesitated.

"Let me just check it over one more time," she replied.

A little extra time and effort, something most of us feel too tired to put in, usually can make at least a little difference, say between pretty good and very good, or between very good and excellent. However, because we don't *want* to do it, we need to raise the stakes and heighten the contrast, so that the difference now is between success and disaster, between getting it right or having to pay your tutor, parent, coach, or sibling ten dollars. This incentive—putting your money where your mouth is—forces our kids to slow down.

Something to Try . . . to Encourage Accurate Self-Evaluation

The betting method does not have to be about achieving perfection. We can agree to whatever standard we want with our children. It's just a matter of asking the "How confident are you that you will reach the standard you set for yourself?" question. To combine this method of slowing your child down while maintaining the enthusiasm and investment discussed in the first chapter of the book, begin by finding out what your child's goal is. Then, get her to consider whether she really has done a good enough job to achieve it.

The dialogue might look like this:

"What are you aiming for?"

"I'd like a B+ or higher. Is that okay?"

"That's up to you—you set the goal."

"Okay, I'd be happy with a B+, and I think I've got it."

"How sure are you?"

"What do you mean?"

"Would you be willing to bet ____?"

You fill in the amount of money or something else, such as doing the dishes for a week, that would let you and your child know that she has considerable confidence in her preparedness.

This method of raising the stakes tends to be most effective when the issue is not about being quick but about achieving a high degree of quality. Since our kids naturally tend to rush, we are giving them a clear reason to slow down.

To Do or Not to Do: How to Build the Habit of Attention

Netflix and YouTube and gaming, oh my! It's not Atari and *Happy Days* anymore—pleasures and diversions from back in the day that were good fun but not designed to absorb us for entire afternoons. Nobody binge-watched *Mork and Mindy*, and even the greatest game of Pong was only enjoyable for half an hour at most. If you watched *Friday Night Lights* or, according to my younger daughter, *Pretty Little Liars*, you will feel unsatisfied when the episode ends because it always ends on a cliffhanger. If you play a video game these days, you often have to continue until you hit a certain level or you will lose your progress; your fellow players will be upset with you and might not let you join their fellowship next time. (I'm not kidding.)

In the social media world, the app Snapchat has "streaks" that track how many consecutive days you have chatted with a person, but do you know how many streaks your child is maintaining on a daily basis? (My younger daughter had about ninety the last time I asked.) What happens if you break a streak? Try walking under a ladder rather than take a chance on this move, since it's guaranteed social suicide. With such well-designed distractions today, it's somewhat impressive that we ever leave our screens. In this Age of Attention, success, and even sanity, depend on developing the will and the skills to focus on what we really care about, and not on whatever is popping up in front of us.

When discussing this topic with my younger daughter, I started by saying that I wanted less friction in my relationship with her over her putting her energy, first and foremost, into productive activities. I suggested that she use a tracking app for key daily habits, including doing her miserable physical therapy exercises, getting chores done, and practicing her Hebrew. She said it wasn't necessary. I told her it would be great because then nobody would have to nag her. It was a win-win.

"It's actually easier if you just remind me," she said.

"No, it's not," I said.

"Really, Dad. It is. Even though it's a pain when you remind me, it is easier. I don't have to think about it."

"I know," I told her, "but it's not easier for me. It's actually a pain for me, too. I need to keep track of my own responsibilities, so I definitely don't have the mental space to keep track of yours on a daily basis. The fact that you are not thinking about it means that I am thinking about it. I also want you to have the skill to do it for yourself."

"But I hate To-Do lists," she said.

"How else could you remember it?" I asked her, trying to be open to the possibility that she had a better idea.

"In my head."

I paused. "Listen, sweetheart," I said, "keeping track of things 'in your head' really is a To-Do list. It's just the *least reliable* To-Do list ever. If that's the To-Do list you want to use, you can, but you'll have to prove it works through your results without any other reminder system, or else you will lose access to things that I think are in the way of your remembering, things such as your phone and your laptop."

"Tell me about this dumb app you want me to use," she said.

Staying focused on a consistent basis, returning again and again to the things that matter to us, requires a combination of willpower and effective tools. I mentioned earlier the app we use called ScreenTime that allows her to earn more phone time if she completes some of the mundane tasks she would otherwise avoid. Of course, it would be and will be great for her to remember and choose to do these things anyway, but the fact that she's doing them is enough for now. At this time, she needs a reward that is both real and of immediate value to her to get the job done, and getting additional phone time is the reward she values.

The app I personally love best for self-monitoring is Habit List. Whether it's a daily habit or just for certain days of the week, the app allows me to add habits, get reminders for them, and check them off. I can see my streaks and weekly stats. I call it my "To-Be" list instead of my To-Do list because I use it for regular things, habits I'm trying to build, not one-off tasks. I use other To-Do apps, such as Wunderlist, for everything from remembering to make a professional phone call to fixing something around the house. I use Habit List, on the other hand, for self-maintenance and to develop consistency in building positive habits, such as meditating daily, having a limited amount of sugar each day, and writing down three things I'm grateful for at the end of the day.

Setting intentions and tracking progress develops fortitude, focused attention, and the ability to overcome internal resistance. Changing daily habits results in actually changing the wiring of the brain, as well as in changing our definitions of who we think we are and what we are capable of. As we see old habits die off due to deoxygenating them, and new ones being formed as we will them into existence, we can feel a certain excitement about what we are accomplishing.

The real payoff comes after we've gone through this process for several habits. At that point, we start to become aware of our capacity in general, our ability to improve as people, perhaps at almost anything. We see that with the proper focus—with the ability to start something difficult, stay with it, and complete the job—we can develop a greater capacity to change elsewhere. Because of this expanded capacity, Habit List is my favorite app. It shows me that I have made major changes in my life, not 100 percent of the time, but 60 percent, or 90 percent, or whatever it is. The key is to make use of something that pushes us into doing what we truly want to do. It's a way right now while we're motivated to influence our futures by programming commitments that will continue to get our attention.

Something to Try . . . to Model Habit-Building

For three weeks, try Habit List, Streaks, or some other way to track your own success at following through on the development of a habit. You can look up "habit builder apps" online and follow links.[58] If you're already doing it elsewhere, such as Weight Watchers, some place where you are consciously and regularly working on a change, that will also do. When you feel that you've achieved a degree of appreciation for the difficulty involved, and for the benefits of cultivating that sort of discipline, tell your child the legendary story of Gandhi who was asked by a woman to tell her son to stop eating sugar. Gandhi told her to come back in three weeks. She did and asked him again. This time, he looked directly at the boy and said, "Son, do not eat sugar. It is very harmful." The woman rejoiced and then asked Gandhi why he had sent her away the first time. He said, "Three weeks ago, I was still eating sugar." Tell your child what

---

[58] See Fast Company's "24 Free Apps to Help You Change Your Habits."

you have been up to in your own efforts at self-improvement. Then, either allow your child to choose their own habit to cultivate, or, if there is something you deem critical, you can explain why it is too important for you to let them not choose it, why it must be an area of focus. Work out an agreement on what your child will do—such as getting out of bed on time independently or offering to do something helpful for the family when you come home from work. Then, come up with a simple system for tracking. Practice may not make perfect, but it will make your child more focused, more confident, and more successful in whatever changes you and/or they deem most important.

Managing attention is a conscious choice. Removing distractions is a prerequisite, but building the right habits is necessary for being able to focus in spite of distractions. As this skill becomes stronger, our children will be able to tackle the more complex challenges that require prioritizing, planning, time management, and organization.

Chapter 5

Learning to Decide: The Executive Suite and Strategies for the Unproductive Child

Every year is getting shorter,
never seem to find the time.
Plans that either come to naught,
or half a page of scribbled lines.
And then one day you find,
ten years have got behind you.
No one told you when to run.
You missed the starting gun.

—Pink Floyd, "Time," *The Dark Side of the Moon*

Introduction: Safe Travels and Perfect Leadership

Imagine that you want to achieve something difficult, such as climbing a mountain or, if that's too easy, too hard, or just plain unappealing, make it a metaphorical mountain and fill it in with another challenge: moving from your current home to another, hunting for a job you're excited about, putting on a great party, or learning a skill, such as piano, tap dancing, or how to file taxes.

One way to approach the task is to wing it. You could just go for it and see what happens. It's less stress to start without any thinking, at least at first, but there are disadvantages. Halfway up your personal Everest, you may realize you've made a huge mistake and decide to turn around, although by then you might be short a finger or two from frostbite. You can chalk up the failure to a learning experience, if you still have enough fingers to write with, but it's a costly way to learn.

Another idea is to plan things out. Approached this way, you research and consult with experts, eventually hiring a guide who has made the trip many times before. You get the right equipment, and you train to make sure that the challenge is one that you can handle. You develop a timeline for starting and for achieving key milestones along the way. You are also flexible, modifying your plan as you proceed based on factors you know you cannot control, such as the weather, and any unforeseen obstacles. You see that preparing ahead of time, staying alert, and making adjustments throughout the experience are essential to your success. You may even come to enjoy the preparatory work itself. In pursuing something great, you feel the joy and excitement of the pursuit itself being done well. You also, having planned intelligently, have the bonus of feeling all those warm fingers of yours that haven't been lost to the grim conditions on the mountain.

These higher-level Executive Function skills of prioritizing, planning, managing time, organizing, and thinking flexibly allow us to avoid many unnecessary setbacks. If we thoughtfully choose what matters and set aside dedicated time to those things, we will not need to work as hard on some of the attention challenges discussed in chapter 4 because we won't waste time elsewhere. If we are skillful at using these Executive Function skills, we will have good reason to be calmer and, therefore, will be less vulnerable to the dysregulation discussed in chapter 3. The most noticeable result is that we will dramatically increase the likelihood of achieving success on big jobs.

This chapter takes a closer look at how to help your child establish priorities, plan out tasks, and get organized to become more efficient. It emphasizes the Teach part of our Reach, Teach, Reflect, Release process as the tools shown can be directly taught once you and your child have the other pieces in place. Once your child is motivated, calm, and focused, and you have learned how to communicate effectively based on the stage of change, they will find it much easier to develop the skills in this chapter.

These higher-level skills will allow your children to navigate the adult world and run their lives relatively independently. Having these basic competencies allows our children to grow into adults who know what their goals are and have the best odds possible of achieving them. Being a good boss of oneself—kind but firm, focused and deliberate—is the essence of possessing and using Executive Function skills well. Whether your children work for someone else (and it's most likely that they will, at least in the short term) or become their own bosses, they will certainly need to manage at least one employee: themselves.

Finally Learning How to Read: Taking Ownership of the Material

My first personal encounter with the DKDK (see chapter 3, "I Do, We Do, You Do") occurred during my first semester of college. Enrolled in a Latin American studies course taught by a great lecturer, I found myself overwhelmed by the reading. Part of it was the unfamiliar content, but the real problem was the sheer number of pages to read. I decided to drop the course, but my professor insisted on meeting with me first. He asked me why I was leaving his class, and I explained it to him.

"How do you read these books?" he asked me.

I think I may have frowned, but I remember exactly what I said. "Well," I began, "I open the book to page 1 and read it. When I'm done, I go on to page 2 and read that. That's my usual pattern."

He ignored my wise-guy tone and said matter-of-factly, "And that's your problem."

"What should I be doing?" I asked. "Turning the book upside-down and reading random pages?"

"It might be more effective," he said.

I raised an eyebrow, and he explained.

"You're reading without thinking, without searching. You need to be like a detective, looking for clues about what's important, spending time on what matters and moving quickly past the fluff."

"How do I do that?" I asked, genuinely interested at this point.

The professor told me that there are a number of ways to read. The default that most students think of is to read "every syllable on every boring page." But if we more finely slice that, we arrive at other possibilities, such as skimming, close analysis, big picture reading of headlines and titles, summary reading at ends of chapters, and so on. Each of these is associated with a particular time and effort factor. The trick is to figure out the type of reading needed for a given assignment. Active reading strategies involve establishing a purpose and focusing on what is important. They involve making decisions about where to direct our attention, and lead to better understanding and stronger retention. These strategies can make a tremendous difference in a student's success, especially in subjects that they do *not* love. Becoming more selective about how to manage one's time in big tasks, such as doing well in a reading-intensive college course, is an Executive Function skill that becomes critically important as our children become young adults who do not have us right by their sides to tell them when enough is enough. Given our children's limited time and attention, strategies like this don't just increase performance by a few points or half a grade; they literally make the difference between staying or quitting. Thanks to this professor, I stayed in the course and even took a second, more advanced class on the topic.

Until our children recognize the deficiencies in their approach, though, they are unlikely to want to learn new ones. They need someone to point out the blind spots and, ultimately, to develop the habit and skill of finding those blind spots for themselves so they can do something about them. The prerequisite is for our children to understand the idea of blind spots.[59]

You can share the analogy of driving. The mirrors cover most of what we need to see, but there may still be blind spots. Even where new car models take care of that particular dilemma, we can talk about the rearview mirror as an example of one view not covering everything. Ask your older child where they get surprised (and disappointed) the most often. Is it in a particular class or on a particular type of assignment? Is it with a particular teacher or type of teacher? This sort of focused question can help eliminate the blind spots as your child learns to take ownership for the material rather than passively hoping it makes sense or, worse, dropping out.

---

[59] For a more extensive look at this, see Meltzer, "Teaching Metacognitive Strategies," *Executive Function in Education*, 275.

> ## Something to Try . . . to Help Your Child Become an Active Reader

Have your child read with a purpose by asking them to show you one sentence in their novel or textbook that is valuable and another that isn't very important. If they can find this sort of contrast, then they are reading actively.

If they're stuck, ask what the purpose of the reading was to begin with. Knowing the purpose changes what matters in the reading. Perhaps the teacher wanted the students to focus on the setting, for example, and not so much on plot development. Perhaps it's a reading for your child to identify vocabulary they don't know and to contribute a few words to the class pool of "new and challenging words." Perhaps it's to answer questions at the end of the chapter, in which case the best strategy is to read the questions first and search for the answers. Bear in mind that as much as you want your child to learn the content of the reading, what you really want is for your child to learn how to be efficient. They will need this Executive Function skill of identifying what matters in all sorts of contexts, not just in a particular book or class.

Getting Cozy with Covey: Principles of Time Management

To be successful on both specific projects and on the much broader project of living their lives fully and successfully, our children need to learn how to prioritize, how to create plans centered on their priorities, and how to execute those plans within the deadlines that the real world imposes on them. In his seminal work *The 7 Habits of Highly Effective People*, Stephen Covey shared a tool (see figure 16) that serves as a strong foundation for deciding what to get done when. His framework helps organize tasks by their urgency—how immediately something must be attended to—and importance, how valuable the activity is.

While this approach does not come naturally to most of us, it is even less intuitive for children. First, they are at the behest of adults who have more power and experience than they do. If a teacher tells a student to do something, it is unlikely to occur to a student, especially a younger one, that the assignment is not particularly important. For kids, it's easy to have the "either/or" thinking of "important/not important" instead of the more nuanced view we have—and the teacher probably intended—that has a whole range, from "interesting to look at if you have time," to "necessary to complete," to "must be done at top quality." In addition, with their less developed Executive Function skills, children may not have learned yet how to distinguish between the two different dimensions of urgency and importance. My older daughter, for instance, though motivated to do her best in school, bemoaned the lack of time she had for a major project in her Spanish class.

"Between the hour a night we have for calculus homework, another hour for history, and another hour that's just for the Spanish homework—plus my theater classes—sometimes we can't even start our projects until the night before! It makes no sense!" she complained.

"Give me the bigger picture," I asked her.

"Well, after getting home between six and ten o' clock because of auditions or rehearsals, plus homework from my academic classes, plus work in my theatre arts classes, I just don't have time to work on a project until the night before. And that's true for everybody!" she said.

I ignored the "everybody" comment, knowing I'd never win that battle, and focused, instead, on her choices.

"How many points are the homework assignments worth that you're doing in Spanish each night?" I asked, suspecting that she was expending too much energy in the wrong places but wanting to hear it from her.

"I don't know. Probably one to two points apiece."

"And the project?"

"Fifty points."

"Oh," is all I said. I was trying to avoid making it obvious that I was going somewhere with this, so she wouldn't shut down the conversation when I clearly had a point I wanted to make, a point about points, actually.

"What?" she said. "I know you're thinking something. Just say it."

"Nothing, really. I was just wondering how much it would cost you, points-wise, if you spent fifty minutes a night on the Spanish homework and put the ten minutes per night you'd be saving into brainstorming and researching for your project."

"I don't know. Probably I'd get about the same grade on the homework. Okay, yeah, I know," she said, somewhat annoyed with me but mostly with herself for her allocation of time, which she could see didn't make a great deal of sense. She was caught in the urgent; I was trying to help her shift toward the important.

"Either way is understandable," I assured her. "It's just that, mathematically speaking, it seems that you'd do better in the class if you took a little time away from the small things and put that time into the one big thing so you don't have to rush on it. You'd also have time to improve it at the end."

"You know it's annoying sometimes having a dad who is an Executive Function coach," she said.

She recognized that her approach to the situation didn't make sense and wanted to put more effort into the project; she just hadn't yet come up with a solution. In talking it out, she came up with the idea of spending forty-five minutes per night on the homework so that she could do a "good enough" job on the nightly requirement, and then have fifteen minutes per night freed up to work on the project. Thus, by the time she reached the final night, she had completed much of the project and only needed to review it instead of rushing to draft and edit the entire thing in one or two days. What made it so difficult to see this in the first place was that she was caught up in tasks that were, indeed, urgent but that were not particularly important. In doing so, she was neglecting a task that was far more important but was not urgent, at least not yet.

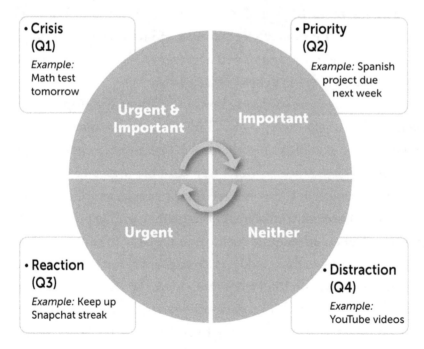

• Crisis
(Q1)
Example:
Math test
tomorrow

**Urgent &
Important**

• Priority
(Q2)
Example: Spanish
project due
next week

Important

Urgent

Neither

• Reaction
(Q3)
Example: Keep up
Snapchat streak

• Distraction
(Q4)
Example:
YouTube videos

Figure 16: Covey Quadrants Framework[60]

---

[60] This tool is also known as the Eisenhower Matrix, as credit is given to our 34th president for inventing or popularizing the first version of it.

As figure 16 above shows, homework assignments due the next day, especially those that might not even be checked for a grade and that the teacher will review in class, are often mischaracterized. Their immediate due date does mean they are urgent. However, the lack of a grade, coupled with the teacher's plan to review them with the class, also means that consequences will be minimal if your child consciously decides to do the work at a basic level instead of aiming for near perfection. These tasks, then, are in the third quadrant, Q3. While it is important for your child to do the homework because he needs to know if he has any questions for class, it would be foolish to spend too much time on this particular task at the cost of working on something more consequential. Homework is generally a "Quadrant 3" activity, urgent and necessary to complete, but not so important that it needs to be obsessed over.

For those assignments that are both urgent *and* important—Quadrant 1, in other words—it is imperative to get busy on them. The point value is high, and there won't be another chance to get them done. Most students don't have trouble understanding this category; it makes intuitive sense. Young people, as well as adults with ADHD, frequently inhabit Q1 because they tend to procrastinate, and they feel an adrenaline rush when they try to complete these high-stakes tasks as the window is closing. Unfortunately, in spite of their feeling a certain high from this kind of approach, work quality suffers. Many things that have become urgent didn't have to be. They could have been planned out had the student started earlier and more methodically.

The trickiest category is Quadrant 2 (Q2), tasks that are important but are not screaming for attention because they are not due right away. These challenges—usually projects due a week or more out—require, first and foremost, an understanding of the slide from Q2 to

Q1, the tendency of people to delay what is not urgent until it *is* urgent, even if it is important. The tool in the next section, "Planning . . . to Get It Done: Basic Project Management Skills," provides an effective antidote to this problem.

The final category, Quadrant 4—that which is neither urgent nor important—is one that most of us, kids included, are willing to concede is not worth our time, but we do these things anyway. What drives us to these non-productive activities? First of all, they're enjoyable; we are hardwired to enjoy certain things like adrenaline challenges (video games), and social connection (social media). These things are the equivalent of sugar, fat, and salt: things we like and that our ancestors needed to get as much as they could for survival, but that we have too much of today.

Not everything that we enjoy is Q4, thankfully. Some things, such as exercise and maintaining strong relationships, are restorative in nature and are Q2, important and only urgent if neglected. Q4 is more like having a lot of wine and a Netflix binge. When we are feeling a bit weak, typically because we have exhausted ourselves from too much time in Q1 fighting the fires of various crises, we are susceptible to retreating to Q4. Often, we created this Q4/Q1 loop because we didn't take care of things when they were Q2 and not yet urgent.

Kids especially lack the maturity to see that they are behind in Q2. The lack of immediacy prevents them from realizing that "objects in the rearview mirror are closer than they appear." By learning how to use the Covey quadrants and classify tasks right away, we can help our children begin to understand why it's easy to get behind on projects. Once they understand the essential nature of projects—that they're easy to ignore but carry a big price tag for doing so—we can teach our children the strategy of backwards planning explained in the next section.

⚙️ Something to Try . . . to Help Your Child Learn to Prioritize

Covey's book is worth reading cover to cover multiple times. If you do what is in there, you will build your own Executive Function skills and get better at knowing how to prioritize, plan, and manage your time. If your child reads and puts into practice the teen version written by Covey's son, Sean, it will also be very helpful.[61]

Alternatively, you could start with the easier task of working with your child to think about point values when it comes to school assignments and having their efforts roughly match how much it will affect their grade. This notion seems anti-intellectual in some ways, putting in effort only where you'll get points, but I stand behind it as an experiment. You and your child are gathering data to see how accurately your child perceives point values and if they translate that knowledge into using their time wisely. Maybe they spend too long on the wrong things because they don't actually know how much the assignments are worth. On the other hand, if they do know, perhaps they are panicky and stuck in Quadrant 3, still trying to please the teacher but doing so on the wrong things, which is rather tragic. If they're going to focus on getting higher grades, they may as well do so more efficiently! Encourage your child to see homework as a chance to consolidate what they learned and to notice any remaining confusion, not as a terrifying trial to prove one's worth to the teacher. Also, encourage your child to put more effort into Quadrant 2 so that they don't spend unnecessary time in Quadrant 1.

---

[61] Covey, *The 7 Habits of Highly Effective Teens.*

Planning . . . to Get It Done: Basic Project Management Skills

One place where having strong Executive Function skills makes people shine is in creating efficient procedures. The specific steps of a project may not be all that hard, but identifying what the steps are, the most sensible order in which to do them, how long each step will take, and how to distribute the tasks over a long period of time—*that* part can be very hard! These kinds of issues sapped the motivation of one of my very bright but disorganized students, preventing him from getting to the work and having the kinds of insights he normally would on a more straightforward assignment. When he said that he was planning to get the work done, he meant "wanting to," but he didn't mean "making and following a thought-through plan."

To shift him from vaguely hoping to succeed to actually design-ing a plan, he needed the "how-to" skills that are weak in those with Executive Function challenges. The first time that we worked together on a big project, I needed to offer a great deal of scaffolding to support him and nearly continuous prompts. We used a tool we call the STM, which stands for steps, sequence, time, and mapping.[62]

For his research paper, we created a shared Google Doc, and I had him begin by brainstorming in bullet form all of the steps he had to complete; he came up with six steps without worrying about the order. (See figure 17a.)

---

[62] I realize it could be the SSTM. Remember it in whichever way works for you.

- Draft paper

- Edit paper

- Topic selection

- Write thesis

- Bibliography

- Make an outline

Figure 17a: STM Steps (pre-prompting)

Then, I asked him prompting questions to get him to recall other steps that he probably knew but were not front of mind, such as, "What else could you do after drafting your thesis to see if there was enough information to write a good paper?"

He replied, "Research?"

"Sure," I followed up. "How would you do that? Where would you go?"

He now had ten separate steps. At that point, I suggested additional steps that I thought would be worthwhile for this project, another two items for the list, and told him to include them for now and remove them later if they proved to be unnecessary. Having bulleted those steps, we then converted the bullets to numbers so that we could sequence them in a logical order, a relative strength of his. (See figure 17b.) He could see, for example, that it was important to draft his topic sentences—the main idea in a given paragraph—before figuring out all of the supporting details.

Next, we put in time estimates for each step, one of the hardest tasks for him. His tendency was to underestimate how long it would take to get things done. As a result, he frequently found himself tight for time, having to stay up late to complete a task and rushing to get

1. Topic selection
2. Rough thesis
3. Research
4. Better thesis
5. Main ideas
6. Supporting details
7. Make an outline
8. Draft paper
9. Revise for organization
10. Add and delete information as needed
11. Edit for grammar and mechanics
12. Bibliography

Figure 17b: STM Sequencing

anything done at all, producing something that would inevitably be low quality. I had twin goals to address in this challenge: first, to provide him with accurate information about how long things actually took, and, second, to increase his estimates on how long he expected things to take.

Seeing that his estimates were unrealistic, I had two choices, both of which were less than optimal: to tell him that he was mistaken and that he should agree with me about the time estimate, or to let him find out for himself that he was wrong. The former might have left him annoyed with me and less likely to take responsibility. The latter would, of course, have some negative consequences, such as a poor grade, but would also likely result in him coming up with some unrelated, but in his mind plausible, excuse for why it happened. Unfortunately, neither case would have led to much learning about why it's important to make good time estimates and how to do so.

Instead, we came up with a range of how long things might take (See Figure 17c.) and then collected data. I encouraged him to widen the range by saying things like, "Wow! That would be really fast if you got it done in five to ten minutes. What if everything went a little bit wrong? How long might it take in that case?" While having this information might not immediately translate into more effective behaviors and better results, it began, over time, to build an awareness of how much time really was required. That awareness taught him to consider that he would need to do something differently to get better and faster results and made him a bit more open to advice.

Of course, some students, typically those who run anxious, overestimate the time needed, sometimes to such an extent that they will not even start for fear of not being able to finish. Coming up with a range of how long a task might take and then checking how long it actually took has a dramatic effect on students in this camp as well. However, with this group, the approach is to push them to extend the *low* end of the time range, gently and sometimes humorously nudging them with hints that encourage pragmatism and chipping away at their defeatist perfectionism. "Yeah, it really could take two hours for that step. Actually, someone could spend five hours on it! But that would probably be going a bit overboard, right? I'm wondering how fast it could possibly be done to be 'good enough' for this stage, which is just a draft outline. Let's keep two hours as the high side, but what could be the very lowest side?"

After writing down reasonable time estimates with this student, I helped him to map everything onto his planner. (See Figure 17d.) We put "DUE" on the due date and counted out the number of days he had available to get the job done. We made sure to cross off days that were not going to be workdays because of sports, family commitments, or "no-way-on-Friday" types of days. We looked at other school tasks and found the total number of days that he had at least

1. Topic selection (5–10)
2. Rough thesis (5–15)
3. Research (30–60)
4. Better thesis (10–15)
5. Main ideas (15–45)
6. Supporting details (1–2 hours)
7. Make an outline (30–60)
8. Draft paper (2–4 hours)
9. Revise for organization (1–2 hours)
10. Add and delete information as needed
    (30 minutes to 2 hours)
11. Edit for grammar and mechanics (30–60)
12. Bibliography (15)

Figure 17c: STM Time

thirty minutes available for working on the project and then added the total time needed to complete all the steps. As we mapped the steps onto his calendar, his enthusiasm for the project grew. Now there was a way to get each step done calmly, without rushing, in a way that made it feel very likely that he would succeed. There were even "catch up" days marked with an X in case things didn't quite work out and he needed extra help. Best of all, he could see that there was no day when the demands were beyond his capabilities.

After completing this project, we were able to apply the same process a couple months later to another project, this time with far less guidance from me. When we completed our work together, I didn't hear from him for a year and a half, until he was midway through his first semester of college. He wanted to know how to apply the process we had used to even longer papers. We made some modifications, and after only two sessions, he again no longer

SUN	MON	TUES	WED	TH	FRI	SAT
	Start	Step 1 (10 mins)	X	Step 2 (15 mins)	X	X
Step 3 (60 mins) Step 4 (15 mins)	Step 5 (15-45 mins)	Step 6 (60 mins)	Step 6 (60 mins)	Step 7 (30-60 mins)	X	Step 8 (1-1.5 hrs)
Step 8 (1.5-2 hrs)	Step 9 (60 mins)	X	Step 9 (60 mins)	Step 10 (30 mins)	X	Step 10 (60-90 mins)
Step 11 (60 mins)	Step 12 (15 mins)	DUE				

Figure 17d: STM Mapping

needed my help. Learning to use effective tools like this improves the deployment of Executive Function skills. While planning was still not a "natural" skill for this young man, because he had learned the relevant skills, he just needed a quick booster to perform well at the new level expected of him in college.

Anything but Not Everything: Accepting Limits, Making Choices

In a pathetic effort to try to make up for the time I'd lost by leaving late for one of my daughter's soccer games, I was speeding. Although I didn't get a ticket, it occurred to me how unfair it was to put my daughter's safety at risk, never mind all the other drivers' safety and my own. It certainly wasn't their fault, so I made the decision to be on time, to be a more courteous driver, and to track my progress on my Habit List app and also on EverDrive, an app that evaluates your driving safety for each trip.

I accepted that I had better allow the laws of physics to apply to me and not try to cheat time by leaving late and somehow expecting to arrive on time. The implications for anyone who may have some degree of ADHD are particularly compelling. While there are occasionally legitimate reasons to be backed up against multiple, competing deadlines, for nearly all kids and for both kids and adults with ADHD, the issue is often a failure to feel a sense of urgency. They will wait until the last minute to get started on things, telling themselves that that they could not have started sooner or that they do best when stressed. If stress is their inspiration, then they tend to wait not only out of habit but also out of a belief that it is necessary. To start too early on a paper, a project, or preparing for a test would be to compromise the sharp thinking and all-out focus they get when they feel motivated by the limited time remaining. Or so they think . . .

In fact, this thinking leads to frequent but unnecessary "surprises" about how much more effort is needed than they had expected. Those surprises are not a surprise to parents and teachers and, later in life, to friends, partners, colleagues, and bosses. They are only a source of surprise to the people with time management issues themselves. These delays also result in exhaustion, in work being of low quality, and often in a diminished sense of self-confidence as they tend to become more convinced that they cannot be timely and organized even if they tried. Failing to meet deadlines makes it harder to start future work, since the previous experience was so unpleasant. As an analogy, consider that it takes some time to register the food we have eaten. If we keep eating until we *feel* full, we will overeat. Likewise, for those with ADHD and other Executive Function challenges, the problem is that they are waiting for a starting gun that, in their case, goes off too late. They are simply not wired to feel the necessary level of concern in time to do anything about it. To be successful, they will have to develop the insight and wisdom to realize that their gut feeling is not accurate. Intellectually, it certainly is difficult to start when we don't know how long things will take, if we are congenitally predisposed to underestimate the difficulty of tasks.

One of my students was working on a research paper; he had a terrific thesis and he'd created an outstanding outline, both of which were huge improvements for him. The next big challenge for him was mapping out the time needed to do the writing and sticking to his self-imposed deadlines. One Friday night, when he'd decided to wait until eight o' clock to begin the work, I peeked at our shared Google Doc thirty minutes later and asked him what time he'd started working. He said he'd been at it for fifteen minutes.

"I'm realizing that this is taking a lot longer than just writing a normal essay," he wrote to me right on the document. "I think it's because I am not writing just to get words down. I am having to get the facts for every sentence I write. I think it will go faster in the analysis section."

This was a time management breakthrough for him. He recognized that his pace varied depending on the nature of the work he was doing. Being aware of that fundamental fact helped him to see the big picture of how long things would take, overall. The ultimate conclusion for him to draw was that what he learned here about one project—that the pace varied and would affect total time—applied to the many projects at school and in his life. In other words, time was limited, so he could do nearly anything, and, with sufficient time, do it well. He just couldn't do everything at a high level. Making choices that would allow him to get priorities done very well and less important tasks simply done well enough would bring him greater satisfaction with less stress.

☼ Something to Try . . . to Teach the Effects of Stress on Performance

Find out what level of stress your child thinks they need to operate best. None? A lot of pressure? A little? Sometimes a physical analogue can help make a point. Give your child two medium-sized glasses of a drink they enjoy that are equally full, preferably something with carbonation. Have your child enjoy one of the glasses as you're talking, letting them know that this is an experiment and that their job in this experiment is to finish the drink in five minutes, which is how long the conversation will take. Discuss with your child the pros and cons of spreading tasks out over time versus getting them done quickly. After they have finished their drink, and when it's a good break in the conversation, tell them they must now try to drink the second glass in five seconds or less. Time them. Discuss the difference in the two experiences. They will likely point out the discomfort of cramming with insufficient time. They might even point out that they spilled and now have a bit of mess. These are great parallels to what happens when we rush on our work. It's uncomfortable, and we make a mess.

Sorting or Hoarding: Organization and Primary Real Estate

Organization as an Executive Function skill is a broad topic, encompassing everything from backpacks and binders to the way one thinks. For the sake of simplicity, I'll focus on the organization of "stuff" here. The skill of organizing one's ideas for problem-solving, for research, for writing, or, indeed, for getting anything complex done, constitutes a book unto itself and has interplay with planning and time management skills as well.

Organization begins with having the right tools and a good space for them. It includes sorting things into appropriate categories. Sometimes, it's about putting papers into the right place; sometimes it's knowing how to organize files on your computer. In both cases, the first question to ask is whether these things are needed now, will definitely be needed later, may or may not be needed later, or won't ever be needed again. The same type of sorting can be done for everyday physical items—from items of clothing to umbrellas and vacuum cleaners. Are they needed frequently, sometimes, maybe later, or not at all?

Whether at school, home, or the office, the next step is deciding where these much needed or relatively not needed items will go. As they say in the realty business, the three things that matter here are location, location, location. It's important for our kids to determine where high priority and/or frequently used things go, where the sometimes important things go, and where the "might be used" things go. It's also incredibly important to clear out the "won't be used" things. This will save you from the embarrassing situation of having documentarians come over to make a film about what a hoarder you are.

If you assist your child in doing the sorting, you may be surprised at how hard it is for your child to throw out things, especially since it might be in subjects they detest. Behind their reluctance is a fear that the teacher might expect them to have it later, and they don't want to be told in front of the class that they have "lost" the paper or file, especially if they could have prevented it. They do not trust their own judgment about what to throw out and will not trust yours much of the time. In some ways, this may show a certain wisdom, since we teach them that it's "better to be safe than sorry" and to listen to their teachers. However, you can mollify their worries by letting them be the ones to decide what to toss/

recycle. Moreover, you can let them keep all that stuff that is in the "might need later" category. The key is to coax your child to keep those maybes somewhere that is not in the way, and to agree upon a later time when stuff will be thrown out, even if it is as late as the end of the school year.

The first step in the process is to choose a location for the important things: a place that is conspicuous, impossible to miss, where your child will accidentally stumble over the things they need even if they don't consciously remember where they put them. This location should be in *primary real estate* for your child, a place he values and sees all the time. For drivers, it might mean placing the keys, wallet/purse, and phone all by the door. In the world of backpacks and binders, it is critical to put homework in the front of a binder or a separate homework folder that is sturdy, stands out, and will not be ignored.

This particular space will need to be cleaned out at the end of the week to stay relevant. These primary real estate spots ensure that important things receive proper attention. Using an organizational method is not just about a clever intellectual scheme to remember; it is mostly about making changes that don't require remembering but simply make it easier for our kids to focus on the right things. By eliminating distractions and by making use of the primary real estate idea, we are helping set them up to do better in the future without trying any harder.

This method can be used not only for managing papers but for our screens, too. The goal is the same, to reduce visual clutter so that our eyes naturally go where we want them to. It starts by having only a few folders for large categories visible at first. For example, your child might have just three initial folders: School, Personal, and Other. Within School, there would be a folder for each subject and perhaps one called College Applications if the student is in high school. Inside of a particular subject would be relevant folders, such as Homework, Notes, Returned Tests and Papers, and perhaps folders based on particular content sections. The other folder inside the School folder would be a folder called Due Now if assignments need to be collected in one spot for later submission into teachers' portals. They will feel less anxious having an organized way to find their documents and not just doing a search.

The best way for them to see the value of being organized, whether for paper or electronic documents, is by conducting experiments and seeing the results. I have found that these small experiments make a big difference. Steve, a sophomore in high school, shoved any papers he had on his desk into his backpack at the end of each class with no plan and with no regard for how crumpled or torn they got. He knew the effects. He would have trouble finding what he needed later, and, if he did find it, it was likely to be crumpled up or missing part of it. He was well aware that completing homework was harder because of his disorganization.

We explored a bit why he didn't take the one minute needed to file his papers before leaving class. Did he not know how? Did he not really care? As it turned out, he did know how, and he had all the right materials. However, he was worried about being late for the next class because it was embarrassing. Moreover, his greatest concern was being late for lunch. In his group of friends, the last one to the table was stuck in the "Loser Seat." The rule was that everyone was allowed to make fun of you there, and you weren't allowed to fight back, or you'd get it even worse. For our experiment, we tried having him get organized for a class that was *not* before lunch. The question we were exploring was how it felt, not just whether or not he could file the paper.

"I tried the experiment!" he announced when we started the session.

"And . . . how did you feel?" I asked him.

"I succeeded. I got the paper filed in. In fact, I got all my papers filed in the right place for the class."

"And . . . how did you feel when you were filing?" I repeated.

"Oh, fine. I just did it, no drama. And I wasn't even close to late for my next class."

So we decided to "level up" and try it in every class except the one before lunch, since that was still too risky. When Steve came in the next week, he let me know that he hadn't done the experiment the way we had planned it. He had, instead, done it in every class, *including* the one before lunch. In trying it out, he found that he could, indeed, file his work and still make it on time wherever he needed to be. He just needed to start the filing right away. Although organization never came easily to this student, he found out that he could do it, that it wasn't particularly scary, and that he actually wanted to do it, much of the time, because he saw the benefit. Reviewing the techniques was helpful, but seeing that there were no negative consequences was essential.

As he found that he was more successful at getting things done, which is the heart of why Executive Function skills matter, he not only lost his anxiety but found himself appreciative of the benefits of being organized.

Something to Try . . . If Your Child's Materials Are Disorganized

Does your child have a key place for key items? Try teaching them about primary real estate and the importance of getting key items in the right place as quickly as possible. A couple of specific examples include:

- Have your child file completed homework in a proper homework folder as soon as it is done.

- Have the backpack prepared in the evenings, ready for school the next day.

- Save old tests and papers in an accordion folder or portable filing box each week in case they're needed for a cumulative test.

- Put important objects in a spot where they can't be missed. This is sometimes called stationing and works best when it would be physically inconvenient not to see the object. For example, you can place an apple pie that you must bring with you on your car seat. Forgetting would be extremely memorable—and is very unlikely.

Looking Inside the Briefcase: Practice Makes Better

Organization is no laughing matter, except when it is. During one of my summers in college, I was training my friend Teddy in how to sell advertising space in a campus publication. We had reviewed the likely scenarios, he had prepared his pitch, all of his materials were organized, and he knew how to handle objections. He was ready to begin meeting business owners with his fail-safe hook, "Have you heard of *Campus Connection?* I'd like to show you something to get your reaction to it." He would then open his briefcase before they responded, take out a sample, and the person would be duly impressed. He would field any questions and explain the various features and their benefits. In moments, they would be choosing an ad just right for them, and Teddy would be the nation's champ.

Meanwhile, I was waiting outside as he did his first solo presentation. After five minutes I was pretty excited. For him to be in there for that long meant that he must have reached the right person, and they were interested in the magazine. But when Teddy came out after another minute, red in the face and breathing hard, I knew things hadn't gone as planned.

"Well?" I asked him.

"Well, I couldn't open the freakin' briefcase!"

One thing we hadn't practiced was *opening the briefcase*. One of the dials may have slipped a bit, so the set numbers in front of him weren't working, and suddenly remembering the code had become impossible. The more he tried, the more frustrated he became, and the more frustrated he was, the more impossible it was for him to think clearly.

Sometimes it's these small parts of a job that can really trip us up. For kids, it's often remembering to bring home the right materials or knowing what the directions are asking them to do. Simple things like this actually aren't simple until they're automatic. These steps need to be anticipated, or the other, more complex skills can't be implemented well. The key is to get to the point where the thinking brain isn't even needed, and muscle memory kicks in. When I was training my friend, I should have had him practice opening the briefcase, both with the numbers set properly and with them out of order. If we had, he would have been able to proceed with the work.

Something to Try . . . When Your Child Has Homework Challenges and You Want to Know Why

Find out your child's Achilles' heel or heels. What are the prerequisite skills they need that prevent them from getting to the deeper work?

For example, consider the Continuum of Homework Problems (figure 18). Does your child trip over any of these steps? Some? All? It helps to determine at what points in the challenge the problems occur.

1. Remembering to record the assignment
2. Recording the assignment accurately or checking posted assignments online for details
3. Bringing materials home
4. Understanding the directions
5. Making a plan for the night, including estimating time needed and the order of assignments
6. Creating a good study environment
7. Starting on time
8. Staying focused, managing distractions and anxiety effectively
9. Taking appropriate breaks
10. Completing all parts of the question and assignment
11. Identifying places where stuck
12. Problem-solving when stuck
13. Making a plan to get unresolved questions answered through extra help
14. Reviewing for quality
15. Filing completed work where it will be easily located
16. Turning in completed work at school
17. Checking online (or with teacher) to see that no assignments are missing

Figure 18: Continuum of Homework Problems

A Bigger Perspective: Meeting the Demands of Authority Figures

My freshman year of college, my anthropology professor beat the heck out of me, metaphorically speaking. Our take-home midterm was tough, and I struggled with it for several days, finishing the morning it was due. When I brought it to the professor that afternoon, she was leaving the building.

"Hi, Professor," I said. "That was a tough one, but I think I nailed it. Here you go."

"Nailed what?" she said. "The exam was due at noon. I can't accept it."

I was confused and checked the exam. "Professor Cruella,"[63] I began, "I don't see a time on here, just a date."

"Sorry you missed it," she said, "but I announced it in class."

"I was sick," I told her (truthfully), "and got the exam from a friend who never mentioned the time."

"I'll have to deduct a full grade," she said, and did, bringing my semester grade just low enough to cross from an A– to a B+ at a college that didn't even have plusses and minuses. The deduction left me with a drop from an A to a B on a report card I'd worked rather hard for. When I took it up with the department chair and, after that, the dean, the advice I got was to decide whether to fight back or to learn from the experience. Given that my natural tendency had always been to fight back, the more challenging choice for me was to let it go and to consider what I could have done differently. I still felt that I was right, but I realized that there were plenty of people who had absolutely no interest in my reasons, however legitimate they seemed to me.

---

[63] I'm not 100 percent sure that's her actual name. It's been decades, and my memory may be failing me . . .

As a young adult in college, to learn from the experience, I needed to override my frustration and consciously decide that the better value was the wisdom, not the grade. I paid a full grade to learn that the absolute responsibility was mine, not my friend's, for knowing when the exam was due and the importance of double-checking expectations. I also realized that I had always assumed that time was a flexible thing, somewhat arbitrary, and that people would understand if someone (me, for example!) was a little bit late. Now, I knew that not everyone felt that way and would extend that sort of leniency.

Being good at time management is more than just being smart about leaving on time instead of checking email on the way out the door. It's also about understanding how other people perceive time and what they expect from us. For our kids in middle and high school, it's especially tricky since they have numerous teachers, each of whom may have different expectations.

The broader task of taking into account the perspectives of others requires so much of our children's Executive Functioning: emotional regulation to manage frustration, cognitive flexibility to step away from their assumptions, and the many steps involved in changing behavior if they decide it's something worth their while to do. We know how much even adults struggle with considering the views of others, but it's easier for us since we have a history of having made significant changes, and know that that there is always another way, and often a better way, to do something. Teaching our children to be open to that possibility encourages them to grow from—rather than just survive—challenging experiences.

Something to Try . . . So Your Child Knows That You Understand Their Feelings When They Fail

Perhaps you had a teacher or boss who didn't fill you with joy but nevertheless taught you a valuable lesson due to your mistakes. What lesson can you share with your own children? The mistakes we made when younger can be extremely valuable to share because our children didn't know us back then; they've only known us as mature (okay, kind of mature) adults. They may be pretty excited to see that we were humbled once, too, that we had adults who kicked our butts and helped us become the decent human beings we are today. I'm not recommending telling them everything we've ever done wrong; that might take too long . . . However, if we level with them, they can know that we're not judging them. We had big struggles with our Executive Function skills when we were younger and sometimes do now as well. We mean it when we tell them that it's normal to struggle and have failures and that things get better. Even if we can't relate to their exact struggles, we can relate to having successes and failures. This sort of humility positions us better to be able to teach our children the Executive Function skills they need and to reflect on what they've learned.

Chapter 6

Deciding to Learn:
The Power of Metacognition

God grant me the serenity
to accept the things I cannot change;
The courage
to change the things that I can;
And the wisdom
to know the difference.

—Serenity Prayer

Introduction: Being Reflective to Become Effective

Life may be the best teacher, but it's not always the fastest. As parents, we don't necessarily like it that way. It's tough for us to watch our kids fail and to trust that someday they'll grow into empathetic, competent adults with a sense of purpose in their lives. It's not just that we're worried about their long-term success in the future; it is also truly painful in the moment to see them unhappy. Whether it's socially, academically, or otherwise-ally, a huge part of us wants them to overcome their problems right away rather than allowing them to learn how to figure things out for themselves.

One practice that is guaranteed to help them become both more successful in the long run and more insightful right away is being reflective. This is the Reflect stage of the Reach, Teach, Reflect, Release process. Being reflective leads to being effective. It serves as an accelerator. Cultivating self-awareness allows us to improve other skills. Whether we are blessed with artistic abilities or mathematical acumen, the gift of gab or athletic skills, we can find ways to capitalize on our talents and passions, so that we improve what we're good at as we work around our liabilities. By being aware of ourselves, we have the master key to both efficiency and improvement. Reviewing our progress and seeing that we are doing well given our current abilities, and perhaps even getting better also allows us to feel satisfied in the moment, not just when we have reached major milestones.

The ability to be self-aware is one that improves with age. While even young children can learn from experience, they are often simply in the moment. They don't have a great deal of experience to draw on, and their thinking tends to be rather concrete. We could try to fix all of their problems for them. For example, we could call the parent of the kid who was mean to our child, or fix our child's homework for her. Having done both of those things, I can attest that it takes a self-discipline rooted in some faith in our kids—and in the learning process—to let some of these things work themselves out. A more effective response would be to coax along our children's deepening understanding of themselves so that they learn from their experiences and become more adept at solving their own problems.

With this guidance, they will gain the skills to do things that adults can do: know what their strengths are and how to capitalize on them; know their own weaknesses and how to work around them; determine realistic goals and set benchmarks for success; and assess accurately how certain they are about their level of understanding. These skills show their increasing maturity.

It can be difficult because kids *don't* intrinsically want to reflect on their attitudes and actions and how they can improve. Their natural tendency is to put "bad" experiences—that is to say, painful ones—behind them because they don't want to confront the pain again. When something painful is over, most kids are not saying, "Gee, I'd like to spend today thinking about what is going wrong in my life. Perhaps a systematic evaluation of my attitudes and actions and the associated consequences is in order!" As with adults at times they want to forget about it as quickly as possible. In fact, kids will typically not even want to reflect on positive experiences, because they don't see the point in analyzing them for insights to be applied going forward. It takes work to constantly improve.

Thus, it also requires tremendous energy and a real decision on *our* part to push our kids to reflect. It is hard to do because they will not greet the opportunity with enthusiasm because it's mentally and emotionally demanding for them. This chapter focuses on how to teach the skill of skill building, the ability to make sense of ourselves so that we can make improvements.

Something to Try . . . to Help Your Child Learn How to Learn

What is one place in your life where you deliberately try to improve yourself? How do you do that? For example, if it's cooking, perhaps you watch a cooking channel or baking show and take notes as you do so. Perhaps you have taken a class where the trainer provides you with direct feedback. Presumably, you taste the food as you are making it to get the right balance of ingredients. After the meal, you make notes on the recipe to change the recipe slightly, or to adjust the cooking process.

All of this is germane to helping your child. If you can do this for cooking, your child can do this for their homework. They can watch videos to get more information or work with a friend, alter what their approaches are, seek input from the teacher, make notes on what worked and didn't, and so forth. All of these practices move them in the direction of becoming a very effective student, one who doesn't just do well but who does better and better all the time. By learning how to improve, your child will be among those who have an accelerated learning curve, something that goes far beyond immediate success to an ongoing ability to consistently improve.

Attribution Theory: Controlling What Is in Our Control

One way to help our children become more successful is to help them understand what the fundamental causes are of success and failure. Attribution theory allows us to categorize the way we explain the behavior of others as well as ourselves. As shown in figure 19, we tend to attribute successes and failures to one of four things: the ability of the person, their effort, the difficulty of the task, plus some degree of luck or environmental factors that we can't explain. What is interesting is that research shows that people naturally tend to attribute the behaviors of others as being based on their personalities and on their effort level. For ourselves, however, we tend to explain our own behavior as being based on how hard the task was, competing priorities, and other situational variables that we don't control. In other words, we tend to not take responsibility for our own failures—and even successes—while we tend to praise or hold others accountable for how they do.

To help our kids—and ourselves—become more effective, we need to turn the formula on its head. Instead of blaming external circumstances, we need to teach our children to focus on what they do control, which is their effort. By focusing on effective effort, they see, for example, how much they benefit from practice, from feedback from others, and from overcoming inertia. The improved results encourage them to try new and more effective behaviors that will become sustainable habits. By choosing tasks that stretch them the right amount, they grow stronger and improve their ability, as well. Of course, there are variables out of their control that will assist or hinder them, but the focus is on what *is* within their control.

Even what many people consider luck can be changed. While there is, of course, randomness in the world and people do not start off with all the same handicaps and advantages, their orientation toward the categories in attribution theory will have a significant influence in how things go for them. For example, in the professional world, people learn that working to develop strong networks improves their exposure to opportunity. Others who don't do this may call it luck, but almost every success story tells us of people who worked longer hours, took risks, and stood back up after repeated failures.

	Internal Control	External Control
Stable	ABILITY	TASK DIFFICULTY
Unstable	EFFORT	LUCK

Figure 19: Attribution Theory[64]

---

[64] The version of attribution theory shared here was proposed by Bernard Weiner. See "Attribution Theory (B. Weiner)," Instructional Design.

Begin by considering attribution theory as it applies to you now and as it did when you were a kid. What is one place where you have struggled recently? What about when you were your child's age? At the time, to what did you attribute your difficulties? How much of it would you now say was a "lack of effort" on your part as a kid?

For your child, to what do you attribute their struggles? How much of it is bad luck and/or task difficulty? How much do you see it as being your child's weaknesses? How much of it do you attribute to effort?

Finally, if your child were being completely honest with you and had no threat of punishment or worries about disapproval, what do you think they would say to explain their various struggles? Would they confess to not putting in their best effort? Would they say that they were confused but were afraid to ask for help? The answers to these questions matter because they reveal the degree of control that your child feels they have over their ability to succeed.

Different Flavors of "Stupid": Learning from Failures

An A ain't bad as grades go, and one of the students I coach had received an A on a physics test. He had lost several points for making what he called "stupid mistakes." He did not want to review the test since the grade was undeniably a good one. While I agreed that the grade was excellent, I felt it was important to review the errors. Calling them "stupid" begged all sorts of questions. Was he tired that day? Was the teacher mean? Did he misread a question or neglect to include the units in his answers? The label of "stupid" left us without a path for improvement or learning, and on the next test, who knows? He might need those lost points.

I asked him, "What *kind* of stupid error?" knowing that he wanted to move on, but that I could get away with pushing him to review his errors since he liked science and was confident in his abilities. I asked if he wanted to "go from terrific to personal best," and he agreed. In this case, using his language ("dumb errors") validated his experience of having to deal with me and the test, and opened the door to a quick and straightforward analysis that would help him going forward.

We discovered various categories of stupid. There were "stupid terminology errors," where he wasn't sure whether "dm" meant decimeter (1/10 of a meter) or dekameter (10 meters, which is 100 times bigger); "stupid orientation errors," where he went bottom-up from the endpoint to the origin instead of top-down from the origin to the endpoint on a graph, saying that the velocity was northeast instead of southwest; "stupid reading the directions errors," where he rounded to the tenths, not the hundredths as instructed; "stupid transcription errors," where he misread the "11.8" on the calculator and wrote "11.5"; and "stupid teacher-being-a-perfectionist errors," where he lost credit for writing "7" instead of "7.0."

What a wide range of stupid errors there seemed to be, and solving each required a slightly different tool. Although it all came down to relatively small details in his case, rather than a failure to understand broad concepts, taking the time to reflect and to name the errors—even with somewhat silly titles—helped make them more memorable for future tests. Doing this sort of reflection allows kids to develop shorthand for easier recall later. With practice, our kids can lead the process and learn how to turn past confusions into future tricks and tools.

Whether they have struggled on a relatively minor issue that we think contains some insights for the future or something far bigger that clearly necessitates some reevaluation, reviewing errors is a central part of becoming smarter. In the short run, our kids develop more insights into the topic at hand; in the long run, they become more thoughtful about the way they approach anything that did not come easily.

Something to Try . . . to Cultivate Insight and Reflection

With your child's permission, carefully review one quiz or test. If you want to go deeper, independently review several of your child's successes and failures, looking for patterns. They're likely to be sensitive to hearing your "in the moment" thoughts, so do it with them out of the room. Unlike at airport security where the rule is "if you see something, say something," try asking your child to take a look on their own at what kinds of patterns they see. Afterward, if your child is open to it, you can trade notes to see what each other thinks. If your child is very sensitive to hearing your observations and feels judged by them, a thoughtful and relatively neutral adult, such as a teacher, therapist, or coach can listen to your observations, share their own, and perhaps bring your ideas forward to your child.

Another approach is to consider what your child would like to excel at, something your child would like to make real growth in and improve their personal best. Ask what they would hold as a personally great achievement in this domain. It could be hitting a ping pong ball back and forth with you twenty-five times without a miss, or it could be something more academic in nature. Regardless of the area, the key thing is to find a reach that is challenging but doable with effort. Ask your child how long they think it will take to achieve this goal.

Once they have achieved this goal, ask how they feel. You may not receive an in-depth analysis, but regardless of their response, you are encouraging something very important: reflecting on successes, not just on difficulties. It can be both satisfying and valuable to see that some choices were helpful along the way while others were more of a hindrance.

Three in a Row: Establishing a Standard for Success

It's interesting how kids evaluate themselves. The claim my student made was that he was "very reliable" at remembering certain formulas in math. I tested him on the formulas and, well, I didn't share his confidence. Instead of discussing the definition of "reliable," which would have put me in opposition to him, I took him outside and shot some baskets with him. He was so happy to take a break from the math that he didn't ask me why. I asked him what his best "go-to" shot was. He dribbled over to just right of the foul line, stopped, and popped. The ball went in.

"Nice!" I said. He smiled. "Now do it again," I requested.

He did it again, and came close, but the ball hit the side of the rim and bounced off.

"Hold on," he said, and did it again, a bit more methodically, and swished it.

"Can you do it three times in a row?" I said.

"Definitely," he told me. Not until five minutes and fifteen tries later had he gotten three in a row. An additional five minutes after that, with a bit of coaching, he could stand in the same spot and get one in with his eyes closed.

I asked him how reliable he wanted to be with this shot.

"Pretty much perfect, while guarded, with time running out on the shot clock, pretty much never miss it," he said.

"What percentage?" I persisted.

"Ninety at home when I'm just practicing," he said.

"So, do you think you have work to do to get there, or are you there already?" I asked.

"Lots of work. I'll keep at it."

We went inside.

"How about the math? How reliable is good enough for you?"

He looked at me. He had done the calculations, so to speak, and knew what I was getting at. "I think for this test, I should be able to give the right formula for any question you ask me, even if I mess up the actual calculations when I solve the problem," he said.

I told him I liked his attitude and agreed that we didn't need to worry about calculation errors right away. So, how did this relate to basketball?

"Well, I can be good at something but still have room for improvement . . . And, I guess I didn't know that I could get better since I thought I was really good at it, so I never really measured my accuracy. But without keeping score, I never found out that I needed to improve. Basically, you definitely have to keep stats to know how you're doing."

This student went on, not only to do a solid job on the test by his own standards, but to be named the best player in the state for another sport during his senior year. Learning to self-monitor, to know what you know and don't know and then to adjust, is at the heart of improvements.

Something to Try . . . When You Want Your Child to Consider a Change

Consider something you want your child to do but that your child doesn't think they need to do. They're in the Precontemplation ("No way!") stage and thinks they're "just fine," and that the problem is yours. Or perhaps your child is in the Contemplation stage where they are considering the issue but not making any headway as far as you can tell. In either case, your child's perception doesn't come anywhere near matching your own awareness that there is an issue and it needs attention.

Try asking, "What would it take for you to come to the conclusion that you need to . . . ?"

Ask for something that may only be in your wildest hopes and dreams, such as, "What would it take for you to decide that you needed to clean your room?" or "to study for tests with at least two days of prep time?" This type of "What would it take . . . ?" question prompts our children to think about the future and not to defend themselves in the moment. They're much more willing to consider the possibility with the theoretical question than if we ask, "How come you haven't . . . ?"

Asking in this way also encourages divergent thinking, thinking in different directions, and the trying on of new perspectives. By asking the "what would it take . . . ?" question, we are not imposing our opinions or even our emotional reactions on our kids. We're just curious what their threshold is for making a change. It's important to ask the question in a way that does not allow for a dodge; for example, if the question is a close-ended—"Could you imagine a scenario where you would need to clean your room?"—the answer may well be "no" because they are not interested in finding a solution in the first place. Never ask a "yes-or-no" question unless you're prepared to accept the response you really do not want. Asking "what would it take?" does not force your child to agree with you on anything in particular, but it does force him to consider the cost he'd have to bear before he would be willing to consider making a change.

When "Help" is a Four-Letter Word: Learning to Self-Advocate

One of the hardest things for kids is going to see the teacher for help. Often, it feels like a waste of time to them. We suggest it, and they say, "Do I have to?" or, "It won't make any difference." At other times, it feels embarrassing because they worry that other kids might judge them or, quite frequently, because they believe that the teacher will be annoyed even if they are professional enough not to say anything. "I don't even know what to ask them," or, "They'll get mad at me," are common responses to suggestions that they go to the teacher for help.

Unlike our kids, we have the good fortune as adults to ignore much of what we don't know about and/or don't care about. If we've never investigated something we find insignificant or confusing, nobody can make us study it! How many bits of information do we take a glimpse of and dismiss because our minds are on matters that we find more compelling? Perhaps we should know more about the political situation in certain countries, or even just attend our town meetings more often. Maybe we should keep up with the big discoveries occurring all the time in science and read the most important literature that is winning Pulitzer Prizes. But do we? No, we're reading books about what's on our minds right now, such as how to help our kids (good for you on that one), getting dinner ready, and trying to still get to the gym, keep the house somewhat presentable, and do a decent job at work. Thankfully, we get to choose.

By contrast, our kids do not have that choice. They are forced to study topics that are not of their choosing and sit next to kids they may not like, and they have a bunch of bosses (several teachers, plus parents/guardians, plus leaders of other activities they attend) telling them what to do. They also feel a great deal of pressure to do well, even on the things they do not understand, and even when they have specific disabilities in those areas. Whether or not they will actually use the skill or knowledge beyond the classroom, they must learn what the school expects or pay a price.

The first step in their overcoming these skill and knowledge gaps and starting to find some meaning in the curriculum is to recognize that a gap exists between what the students know now and what they need to know. Then, students have a reason to seek help. Without identifying these points of confusion, students are typically averse to going to teachers for support. Sadly, it's as common for students to avoid seeking help as it is critical that they do. When we ask students why, we tend to hear the following responses:

"I forget."

"I don't like it. It's a waste of time, mine and the teacher's. Plus, the teacher doesn't like me."

"I don't know what I'd say. The teacher will think I'm dumb because I'll just say something like 'I don't get it.'"

Kids regularly report that the biggest obstacle to going for help is not knowing why they are going. In fact, our kids are correct that it wastes the teacher's time to have a student show up and just say, "I don't get it." It makes sense that the student will then feel somewhat ridiculous. However, if the student has prepared ahead of time and has a fairly good idea of what it is that they don't "get," then the help sessions with the teacher are focused and more enjoyable. The teacher gains respect for this student who clearly cares enough to come prepared, and the student can see that the teacher is enthusiastic about helping them. The experience improves their relationship and opens the door for future help. Finally, the improved grades that are likely to follow prove to the student that getting help when needed is worthwhile.

The DKDK tool discussed earlier prepares students for these help sessions. With this tool, our kids identify what they know (K), don't know well (DK), or didn't even know they didn't know (DKDK). By identifying those blind spots, they feel a sense of purpose instead of dread at the prospect of seeking help from their teachers.

Something to Try . . . So Your Child Sees the Value of Going for Extra Help

Teach your child the concept of the DKDK, and use it with them for something they're interested in, such as an application to a summer camp, or how they'll prepare against another team in a hockey match. There's what they know or believe will be easy (K), there's what they don't know well or believe will be tough (DK), and there are the "surprise" factors that may come into play (DKDK) and what they can do to be ready for them. An adult can be especially useful in helping generate the DKDK part of the list, since, by definition, the kids don't necessarily know what they don't yet know there. See if your child is interested in hearing about some of these unknown-to-them variables and has one of those "aha" moments from something you share. Then, encourage them to use this evaluation tool to prepare for a meeting with a teacher and to see whether it makes a help session feel more worthwhile.

Tracking Progress: Committing to Self-Evaluation

The skill of self-reflection is such an important one that many businesses ask their employees to show evidence of their capacity to do so as part of their performance review. When I ran a school, we counted employees' self-evaluations as part of their overall rating and pay raises. Knowing that someone could not only do a good job but could see their own strengths and challenges gave supervisors a good deal of confidence in the person's ability to continue to improve.

Self-evaluation is used in all sorts of professions, such as sports. Professional athletes watch tapes of previous games not only to scout their upcoming competition but also to see how to improve in the next game.

For the past twenty years or so, I've been playing Ultimate Frisbee, a sport where, at most levels, players call their own fouls and, in the adult leagues where I've played, don't have a coach. As a result, there aren't formal opportunities for feedback. However, many players have devised their own personal scoring systems to track their performance. For example, you gain an individual point for scoring as a passer or receiver and lose a point every time you make a poor throw that results in turning the disc over to the other team.

Keeping this personal score matters to many of the best players, who not only want to win the game, but who want to focus on their own continuous improvement. One player I knew had a habit of attempting passes over distances well beyond his range. Other players, myself included, kept telling him to be more conservative and to make better choices. To the annoyance of his teammates, he didn't listen, and every time he succeeded with one of his prayer throws, he'd feel so good that he would refer back to it the next five times when he missed. Unfortunately, in this sport, losing possession because of a bad pass is costly, and completions should be made at least 90 percent of the time. Unfortunately for new players, the intermittent reinforcement of winning a point is such a rush that almost everyone takes more risks than is reasonable when they start off.

With this newish player, I mentioned the self-scoring method taught to me. He decided to try it and, to nobody else's surprise but his own, his scores were initially in the negative numbers. He started to pay more attention to the cost of his risky decisions, and, after just one week, he rarely attempted the big throws. When he did, it was with better judgment when he was far more likely to succeed. In fact, one time, when he took the risk against his own better judgment, he was so disgusted with himself that he voluntarily gave himself a –2 instead of a –1. With this kind of focus and orientation, he rose to a much higher standard. This type of personal scoring can help our kids become reflective and effective.

⚬ Something to Try . . . to Build Self-Assessment Skills

Work with your child to design your own self-scoring system on something and put it into practice. An easy example would be getting homework done. Your children may have very different ideas from you about what it means for them to do a good job on their homework. Begin by coming to an agreement about how you define "good." Which categories matter, and what are the criteria for each? The rubric in figure 20 is an example, but you can modify it in any way that allows you to have a common understanding of what is good enough. Having a personal score for something like homework also allows for tracking and analysis. Perhaps one aspect, such as planning, is going well, but quality is subpar. With a bit of data, which will likely require our guidance, our kids can see how they're doing and how to improve.

	2	1	0
Timing	Made plan right away. Stayed on schedule.	Didn't make plan but got done with plenty of time.	Poor planning, rushed, stressed, done late at night.
Quality	Shows hard work and doing at least as much as the teacher wanted or going beyond.	Got the job done. Will get full credit.	Seems to show lack of effort and will not get full credit.
Prioritizing	Plan made for long-term assignments, allocated appropriate amount of time for nightly work.	Nightly homework done reasonably efficiently. Long-term assignments not addressed.	Too much time spent on 1–2 things and others, especially harder things, entirely neglected.

Figure 20: Rubric for Homework

The Costs and Benefits of Procrastination: Considering Consequences

Since he had not posted his weekend homework on our shared Google Doc that kept him focused, I was unable to tell if my student was up to date or not on completing his assignments. The reckoning happened on Monday when his mother heard from two different teachers about missing work. She let me know right away. As a veteran mom, she knew not to freak out, and as a veteran coach, I saw a big opportunity. Especially once he confessed that he deliberately did not enter his homework assignments on our shared document because he knew I would hold him accountable, I figured that this was a prime chance to build some reflection skills.

We had three tasks. First, he had to get the overdue work done. The second thing was to understand what happened, why he didn't do it. The third was to be really clear about the negative consequences that came from his decision. Knowing all of this would make it far less likely to be a problem next time.

We scheduled the make-up work for various time slots that afternoon and evening and then did a cost-benefit analysis of delaying the work. The "benefits" turned out to be singular, just one: He didn't work on the weekend and got to avoid an unpleasant task. I persisted in trying to find additional benefits, but he couldn't come up with any. Delaying the pain and having immediate fun were it.

I asked him about the costs.

He said, "Well, I can only get half the credit now."

"Anything else?" I asked. "Sometimes there are hidden costs, and if we close our eyes hard enough or stay busy enough, we can ignore them for a while. Unfortunately, they're still there."

"I don't know," he told me.

"Did you think about it during the weekend," I inquired, "or were you able to go the whole weekend without thinking about it at all?"

"Oh, no. I thought about it," he said. "A lot!"

"How many times? A lot as in two to three times or a lot like eight to ten?"

"A lot as in twenty to thirty!" he said.

"Wow!" I said. "That is a lot. How did you feel when you thought about it?"

"Really anxious and guilty. I knew it was wrong not to do it, and it didn't go away. Also, I knew my parents would be really annoyed, and I would be disappointing my teacher."

"That sounds pretty miserable," I reflected to him. "It also just makes you feel badly about yourself, like, 'I'm the guy who puts things off,' and it makes it harder to do it right the next time. It's kind of building a habit that you don't want!"

He had just named seven different ways he'd screwed things up for himself, and, for the most part, had come up with the reasons himself. And then I reminded him.

"So," I said, "if you want, you can pretend not to notice all of those consequences. That will keep you stuck creating the same problems for a very long time. But once you open your eyes, it's pretty hard to avoid seeing the situation for what it is, which is miserable."

He nodded. This was not the type of situation that he would let himself slip into quite as easily next time. In the Contemplation stage of the change model, we focus on building this awareness skill, the skill, specifically, of noticing the cons of making poor choices. We help our children see that as hard as it is for them to face certain things, it's even harder for them when they don't. Reflecting on the situation and really looking at all of the costs will help them make better decisions in the future. For the change to be long lasting, the person can't just go through the motions; to be motivated, they must see the many reasons why it's worth it to change.

Something to Try . . . to Show the Costs of Procrastination

Try asking your child why they are postponing something, and be genuinely curious about their reasons. This means skipping any of the "shoulds" and other judgmental language and, instead, just asking questions and restating what you think you've heard. That's a whole lot of "So what you're telling me is . . ." instead of "How could you!" In fact, if you feel like there might be an exclamation mark in your voice at all, try saying it again in a way that shows that you're just asking clarifying questions, not preparing to send your child away for twenty years for bad behavior.

Follow up with asking what the costs are and put their responses on a shared Google Doc or some other place you can refer to later. Begin with your child generating the list, and then suggest additional reasons that you feel are relevant. If your child doesn't agree with your reasons, you can still jot them down with a notation that shows your child's opinion, such as, "Mom's opinion is that Zack gets exhausted when he gets behind and tries to catch up. (Zack disagrees.)" These differing views are worth revisiting as points to explore when the next similar situation comes. No end-zone dances for parents when we're right, though—we're on their team.

Self-Talk: Learning from Thinking Aloud

My younger daughter, Eliya, told me that her math homework had suddenly become much easier after her friend Sarah explained how to solve it. I asked her if she had only gotten the answers right or if the process actually made sense to her. She said, "After Sarah showed me, I could explain the problem to myself out loud, and all of the steps made sense."

Self-instruction and self-talk are effective means for us and our children to make sense of and learn from experience.[65] Simply put, self-talk is the mental processing we do at a conscious level; it allows

[65] Zimmerman, "Models of Self-Regulated Learning," *Self-Regulated Learning and Academic Achievement*.

us to understand intellectual concepts as well as to monitor and regulate our emotions. For my daughter, now that she knew how to solve the problem, she could leverage her success to approach her math more effectively next time with far less anxiety. She could not only talk herself through a particular math problem but also think through the process of dealing with other types of problems that were hard for her. Her realization was, "Here's what I can do. I can begin by learning from a trusted friend. Then, I will be able to put the concepts into words that make sense. If I get nervous, I will slow down." The self-talk we do before, during, and after succeeding allows us to remember and utilize our insights again and again, applying them to an ever-wider array of applications.

One reliable way to reinforce our children's learning is to have them paraphrase their thinking into the simplest language possible and then to teach it to somebody else. If they are unable to explain it to someone who knows less than they do, such as someone younger, the chances are that they don't really understand it particularly well. Teaching our kids this principle—that if they have a hard time explaining something, then they probably still have confusion—helps them to develop some self-awareness, a way to recognize when they are stuck.

Teaching our children this approach with self-talk can be equally effective. Children can present the material to themselves as if they were the younger person in question. Wonderfully, if they can make it super simple for themselves, then they probably have a decent handle on the material. They can include illustrations in their explanations, and they don't have to be brief. They simply have to be clear and straightforward from start to finish. Each piece in the chain of logic must be clear and connect properly to the next piece. If your child can do that, then they can be confident that they are in good shape.

Something to Try . . . to Harness the Power of Self-Talk

Find a quiet place to try a bit of self-talk as you complete a task or try to figure something out. Say aloud what you're thinking, what the steps involved are, what errors you observe yourself making and what procedures you carry out that make sense. You're not talking to yourself because you're crazy (not because of this, anyway!); you're just conducting an experiment.

What goes through your mind while driving, getting things ready for guests to come over, or helping the kids get organized in the morning? Can you articulate what the job is, what the parts are that must be completed, what order to do them, and what step you are on now? Do you have a way to recognize if you are off track? If so, you are using a number of skills here, such as cognitive flexibility (jumping from the big picture to the details and back), working memory (holding a bunch of items in your head at once), and the planning skill of sequencing. These are important Executive Function skills.

The next time your child tries to solve a challenging problem, ask them this question: "How did you know that?" When they try to articulate their logic, they are more apt to see the specific gaps in their thinking. Even for problems that they get right, they may not be able to name what they did at first, but over time, they will start gaining the ability to put words to their insights. This type of self-awareness will allow them to replicate her efforts in the future and to apply this problem-solving skill elsewhere. Thoughtful self-talk leads to self-knowledge.

A great way to teach your children self-talk is by modeling it yourself. How do you respond to crazy multitasking challenges such as . . . cooking a meal? Yep, that sort of seriously complex task can be talked about in terms of process. "I'm going to heat up the stove now because it takes a while to get warm, then chop up the vegetables. Hard veggies go in the pan first since they take longer to cook, and I want everything done at the same time . . ." Whether it's shopping for groceries, fixing a toilet, or planning a party, anything that involves multiple steps can provide your child a window into your thinking. Letting your child see how you handle these things when you're confused (beyond yelling choice words), how you decide when to take breaks and when to return to the work, and how you make the many other decisions in the process allows them to learn not just what to do, but how to think.

Self-Discipline: Holding Oneself Accountable

A student I'd been working with for several months was starting his junior year of high school and wanted to end his parents' system of having him gather teacher signatures each week to show his progress in each class. I told him that we had two options: one was to ask his folks if we could waive the requirement with the understanding that we would reinstate it if he was doing badly; the other was to tell his parents that he would start the year with the plan in place but to tell them that if he did well, he wouldn't need it anymore.

When I asked him which choice sounded better to him, he chose the latter. To his credit, instead of asking for an unearned privilege that would have left him anxious about failing, he chose to prove himself first and to operate from a position of strength. He received all As that quarter; and, to my surprise, when I asked if he then wanted to end the signature page, he decided not to end it, just to reduce it to every other week. I was impressed that he didn't want to simply eliminate something he had once complained about as being a "super fun burden with the bonus of a stigma on top." Upon reflection, and now that he was allowed to make his own choice, he realized that the tool provided him with valuable information at a relatively low cost, and that he was content to reduce its usage a bit without eliminating it. This kind of maturity is what we're all aiming for with our kids. Whether we are coaches, teachers, or parents, we want them to make decisions that demonstrate an appreciation for competing values, such as freedom and accountability, in a way that gets the best of both worlds.

⚙️ Something to Try . . . to Gain Buy-In

Consider telling your child that you need to talk about something that is both a choice and not a choice. When they understandably ask you what you're talking about, explain that they need to choose something for which they'd like to be held accountable; however, they will get to choose what that thing is. Furthermore, you will not be judging them or imposing any consequences based on their results. You simply want them to have the experience of gathering data, so they can make informed decisions about what they want to do.

My younger daughter's use of the ScreenTime app (see "Scream-Worthy Screens: How to Tame the Beasts" in chapter 4), the one that limits her use of apps, was a good example for me. One of the best things that happened in addition to us not arguing constantly about whether she could or could not use her phone was that she learned how to pace herself, in this case managing her phone time as others would manage precious food rations on a life raft. She simply doesn't want to run out of phone time at all and, with practice, has gotten rather good at managing herself so that she doesn't run out of time unexpectedly. She manages to get what she wants and to be more mindful of what she is doing. Just recently, she said, "I use my phone more conservatively now. I don't just mindlessly scroll Instagram anymore and usually use it for things I actually care about." Mission at least partly accomplished.

Reflecting on Reflection: Being Satisfied with Current Best Thinking

This same daughter recently had her "Mexico moment," as my older daughter, Jenna, did years ago. Eliya had always been afraid of rollercoasters and had worked her way up gradually to riding any coaster except the ones with loops. Loops remained an absolute deal breaker, un-bribable, even. When my wife chaperoned a field trip to a nearby amusement park, my daughter's friend didn't want to go on coasters that even my daughter liked. Of course, this had the effect of making my daughter feel brave, and before they knew it, they were at the front of the line of the corkscrew with Eliya having some hesitation in her head but committed not to show it. Immediately after the ride, she said two things. First, she said, "Let's do it again!" and second, she told my wife, "You should have made me do it!"

It's funny being a parent, isn't it? We're not often told directly that we were right, and, when we are, we're now the idiots who should have forced our views on them in the first place. When she came home and also told me that I should have made her do rollercoasters, I laughed, knowing that I can't make that child of mine do practically anything, let alone something that I don't particularly care about. I reminded her that she loves how much choice we give her, so hopefully she'll remember this experience the next time that we strongly encourage her to be open-minded about something. The good news, we pointed out, is that she only missed about seven years of great riding. What if it had been a lifetime of missing out . . . ?

She could have given me a sassy look for reminding her of how many fun things she had missed because she had been so resistant. She could have gotten mad, but she didn't. I think it's because my wife and I don't have a great stake in the details of what our kids choose, just that they learn from their experiences and make thoughtful choices going forward. We've found that by encouraging them to reflect on their decisions and the consequences that followed, they make better choices over time. By "better," I mean that they themselves agree that they are more successful and are satisfied that they are making good decisions based on what they know at the time. They at least can say, in the words of Taylor Kitch's immortal character Tim Riggins on *Friday Night Lights*, "No regrets."

Conclusion

I t bears repeating that it's harder to help the kids we care about when they are our own children, when we are their parents (or other full-time guardians) than when we are professionals who can say goodbye at the end of the day. Especially when we have seen the same thing happen over and over again with our kids, it's hard as a parent to avoid feeling responsible for our children's behavior. If we didn't prevent a problem we thought was likely to occur, we may wonder if we should have intervened, removed obstacles, prevented the pain, and kept everyone happy.

Unfortunately, solving problems for our children often creates more issues than it fixes. We don't allow our children to develop their own Executive Function skills, skills we know they will need. We also convey an attitude that life should be smooth and is more about getting things "right" than about learning, growing, and improving. Worse, it sends the message that we don't really trust our kids. They internalize our lack of confidence in them, and as their self-confidence erodes, they become less willing to take chances, to push themselves, and to find out just how much they are capable of.

We want to and need to get to the Release stage of the Reach, Teach, Reflect, Release process with our children, but it's scary and difficult to know just how and when to do so.

I wrote this book because I know that sometimes it's really hard for us as parents who love our kids so much to believe that they will be okay. Some days it will feel as though it is always hard, has always been hard, and will be hard forever. While there certainly are tough moments, it is helpful to frame them as moments that will pass. With a healthy perspective, we may find that they can pass with a bit less pain, a lot less blame, more insight, and even gratitude for the chance to be there with our kids through these once-in-a-lifetime moments.

A family I am close with is fortunate in that both parents are tremendously thoughtful people and understand children very well. They just happen to have one child who has a number of struggles, and it's been hard for all of them. While hiking with them recently, the child tripped while crossing over a long and deep pool of mud and lost his shoe. Considering how aggravating the situation was for him, he did rather well to just shout out a couple of things that I cannot print in a book as polite as this one. Everybody in our hiking group wondered if he would turn back, but with a few kind words from his father, he put his muddy shoe back on and started back on the trail. He completed the hike, through the rain and through his boredom. An hour later, his father slipped and landed in mud and shouted out the same expletives. This time, the son did not fall. His father turned to him and said, "You're doing better than me now!" The kid looked at his dad and said, "Dad, you're gonna be okay." It's a beautiful thing when our children find ways not only to talk to themselves but to talk to us, to see that they are internalizing the best of us.

Raising kids has given me both more daily challenges than I expected and much deeper rewards than I could have hoped. I have, like this couple, had the true blessing of seeing my kids echo the best of my spouse and me and also teach me things that have made me a better person. I wish the same for you with your children.

Enjoy the journey,

Michael

Acknowledgments

I t's such a rare opportunity to thank people publicly in a way that has more shelf life than social media posts, that I've found this part of the book to be the hardest to write. I'm certain to regret having omitted important people. Still, I'd rather acknowledge some of the many people who have been helpful than none, so here goes.

Jackie Stachel, my Director of Marketing and Communications, has been a consistent cheerleader, coach, and friend. Pete Vogt, my Director of Sales, helped me find a title for the book that really means something to me. Both Jackie and Pete convinced me that it would be worth the effort it would take to write a book since we could then provide support to the many families who want guidance but do not have access to our one-on-one coaching services. Of course, I noticed that neither of them volunteered to write the book, but, hey, good idea. Stuart Horwitz, my developmental editor, provided several rounds of phenomenal feedback, ensuring that "Your Kid" would be honest and accessible. The book is several degrees less pompous than it would have been without Stuart's honest notes and conversation. Hire him if you're writing your own book. My beta readers, Kelly O'Leary Schultz and Elizabeth Wilcox, also provided invaluable feedback on a host of issues. Their brilliance and integrity are much appreciated. My copy editor, Sarah Colwill-Brown, was also helpful in this process.

Having a wonderful company that runs smoothly has been a tremendous blessing and provided me room to write. In particular, my right-hand woman, COO Rachel Krompinger is as perfect a leader as I could possibly hope for. She, Operations Manager Tricia Butler, and CFO Larry Kramer, among others, have kept the Beyond BookSmart ship moving in the right direction during the past twelve to eighteen months when I've had the Do Not Disturb sign up. Our professional development experts, Laura Moy and Annabel Furber, have provided me with thoughtful ideas throughout the writing. Laura also gave the manuscript a final read-over that prevented those embarrassing tyypos[66] that can crop up in even the most carefully polished work. I also appreciate the reliability of my assistant, Monique Manna.

I have benefited from a committed Board, including Brian Kessler, Gary Levine, Bob Howard, and Ellen Braaten. They, and the others who have shown faith in me and in Beyond BookSmart, have made it possible for us to achieve this next step in our mission to help anyone who needs it learn the tools and strategies to become more effective and successful through the development of Executive Function skills. A special thank you to Larry Charles and Kathleen Park for being my first investors and, likewise, to Stuart and Dottie Feinzig.

Dr. Penny Prather, Neal Elliott, and Dr. Ellen Braaten have my particular gratitude. Penny was not only a reader who gave valuable feedback on the Executive Function Overview section, but was the first person to encourage me to orient my coaching practice toward the Executive Function skillset. Neal was the first person to provide

---

[66] Couldn't resist.

me with valuable insights about kids with learning differences and to teach me, beginning in 2002, when he noticed that I was a well-intended school principal but had gaps in my knowledge. Ellen and our mutual friend, Jackie Johnson, were the first to tell me years ago that I actually owed it to the world to write a book. I didn't know that that was what I owed the world, nor that the world would agree with their assessment, but their encouragement emboldened me. Another note of gratitude to our original COO, Melissa Doody, who, along with Neal, worked unreasonable hours in the early days of our startup to help launch Beyond BookSmart.

Dr. Ed Zadravec and Dr. David Gleason provided insights and reading recommendations both during my years as a school princi-pal and since then that have influenced my thinking. The writings of both Drs. Peg Dawson and Richard Guare, and of Drs. James and Janice Prochaska have enlightened me, and I have been fortunate to have had quality time with them as I continue to learn from them. Mentoring from the effervescent Steve Levy and the irreplaceable Charles Sposato buoyed my spirit and taught me meaningful lessons when I was a school principal. Coaching from Kerri Yates and Todd Williamson gave me direction and thoughtful processes in the early stages of developing Beyond BookSmart that continue to reap results.

A shout-out to the many friends who have been so encouraging along the way, with a special one to Dan Lewis who buoyed my con-fidence as a writer on a particularly angst-filled day. I am grateful to my friend Laura Basili, who has always taken such a keen interest in my work and has been an abiding source of love and wisdom. To my oldest friend, Barry, thanks for being there from the beginning. To our amazing, twenty-years-and-going-strong book club friends, past and present, thank you for constant encouragement, interest in my work, great discussions, ridiculously delicious meals, and, espe-cially, for continuous friendship. Another shout-out to my friends at

Ultimate for the sanity *and* insanity you help me maintain each week in about the right proportion. Thank you to my siblings, Deb and David; my step-mom Ginger; my in-laws, Sharon, and the Peterson clan, Kol, Thad, Justine, Josh, and Vicki; and the amazing Howards, Michael, Inara, Susan, Brandy, Matt, Bob, and Marge for the ongoing love and support and good times that make life so rewarding. I really lucked out.

My father-in-law, Bob Howard, gets his own byline for being a friend, mentor, and in-law who has advised and supported me in developing both the charter school and Beyond BookSmart. He has had the wisdom not only to impart good ideas but to be patient enough with me to wait until I start to believe the ideas were mine to begin with. He is a model human being.

I am truly grateful to the students I have taught and coached over the years. They have consistently shown courage to grow, and their trust in me means everything to me. Their families have also been an important part of the process . . . and for similar reasons.

A special thank you to my father, who may have embarrassed me as a child by bragging about me to people (we're talking strangers in supermarkets), but whose love for all his children and now grandchildren is limitless.

Finally, to the most important people in my life, my children, Jenna and Eliya, and my wife, Stephanie, there are no words to describe how much joy and meaning my life has because of the three of you. Jenna, thank you for reading the entire manuscript and letting me know that you actually laughed a few times. You are a light that shines so brightly, not just because of your talent, but because of the depth of caring you bring to everything you do. Eliya, thank you for giving me plenty of material for the book (haha) and for being both my mini-me and a true original. The world is a better place because of you. I am blessed by the two of you and grateful to be your dad.

And, Stephanie, my partner in crime—our kids are okay and then some. I am grateful for your warmth, brilliance, and absolutely needed perspective. Every single day, I feel fortunate to be married to you.

Bibliography

Arkowitz, Hal, William R. Miller, and Stephen Rollnick.
*Motivational Interviewing in the Treatment of Psychological
Problems.* New York, NY: The Guilford Press, 2015.

Armstrong, Thomas. *Neurodiversity in the Classroom: Strength-Based
Strategies to Help Students with Special Needs Succeed in School
and Life.* Alexandria, VA: Association for the Supervision and
Curriculum Development (ASCD), 2012.

Barkley, Russell A. *Executive Functions: What They Are, How They
Work, and Why They Evolved.* New York, NY: The Guilford Press,
2012.

Bidwell, Allie. "Most College Students Don't Graduate on Time."
December 1, 2014. National Student Clearinghouse Research
Center. https://www.usnews.com/news/blogs/data-mine/2014/
12/01/report-too-much-freedom-hurts-college-graduation-rates.

Braaten, Ellen, and Brian Willoughby. *Bright Kids Who Can't Keep
Up.* New York NY: The Guilford Press, 2014.

Chua, Amy. *Battle Hymn of the Tiger Mother.* New York, NY:
Bloomsbury Publishing, 2011.

Covey, Sean. *The 7 Habits of Highly Effective Teens.* New York, NY: Touchstone Press, 1998.

Covey, Steven. *The 7 Habits of Highly Effective People.* New York, NY: Simon & Schuster, 1988.

Dawson, Peg, and Richard Guare. *Executive Skills in Children and Adolescents: A Practical Guide in Assessment and Intervention.* New York, NY: The Guilford Press, 2004.

Diamond, Adele and Kathleen Lee. "Interventions Shown to Aid Executive Function Development in Children 4–12 Years Old." National Institutes of Health. August 23, 2011. https://www .ncbi.nlm.nih.gov/pmc/articles/PMC3159917/.

Doran, G. T. "There's a S.M.A.R.T. Way to Write Management's Goals and Objectives." *Management Review* 70, no. 11 (1981): 35–36.

Dweck, Carol. "The Power of Believing That You Can Improve." Filmed September 2014 in Norrkoping, Sweden. TED video. https://www.ted.com/talks/carol_dweck_the_power_of_ believing_that_you_can_improve#t-6865.

Emerson, Ralph Waldo. *Letters and Social Aims.* London: MacMillan & Company, 1883.

Faber, Adele, and Elaine Mazlish. *How to Talk So Kids Will Listen and Listen So Kids Will Talk.* New York, NY: Scribner Classics, 1980.

Fay, Jim. "Two Ways to Neutralize Childhood Arguing." Love and Logic. Accessed January 19, 2018. https://www.loveandlogic.com/ articles-advice/two-ways-to-neutralize-childhood-arguing.

Galinsky, Ellen. *Mind in the Making: The Seven Essential Life Skills Every Child Needs.* New York, NY: Harper Collins, 2010.

Gardner, Howard. *Multiple Intelligences: New Horizons in Theory and Practice*. New York, NY: Basic Books, 2006.

Gibran, Kahlil. *The Prophet*. New York, NY: Alfred A. Knopf, 1923.

Gleason, David. "Expecting Our Kids to Behave Like Adults." *Developmental Empathy* (blog), October 15, 2017. http://developmentalempathy.org/executive-functioning-in-children/

Gleason, David. *At What Cost? Defending Adolescent Development in Fiercely Competitive Schools*. Boston, MA: Developmental Empathy, 2017.

Gray, Peter. "How Does School Wound? Kirsten Olson Has Counted Some Ways." *Psychology Today* (blog), June 28, 2011. https://www.psychologytoday.com/blog/freedom-learn/201106/how-does-school-wound-kirsten-olson-has-counted-some-ways.

Greene, Ross, and Stuart Ablon. *Treating Explosive Kids: The Collaborative Problem-Solving Approach*, New York, NY: The Guilford Press, 2006.

Harvard Extension School. "The Surprising Reason We Don't Keep Our Resolutions (and How to Overcome It)." Accessed January 19, 2018. https://www.extension.harvard.edu/inside extension/surprising-reason-we-dont-keep-our-resolutions-how-overcome-it.

Haynes, Chris. "Curry Calls $50K Fine an '"Expensive Mouthpiece Toss."' *ESPN*, October 24, 2017. http://www.espn.com/nba/story/_/id/21138440/golden-state-warriors-stephen-curry-surprised-amount-fine-tossing-mouthpiece.

Instructional Design. "Attribution Theory (B. Weiner)." Accessed January 21, 2018. http://www.instructionaldesign.org/theories/attribution-theory.html.

Kabat-Zinn, Myla, and Jon Kabat-Zinn. *Everyday Blessings: The Inner Work of Mindful Parenting*. Boston, MA: Hachette Books, 1997.

Kegan, Robert. *In Over Our Heads: The Mental Demands of Modern Life*. Cambridge, MA: Harvard University Press, 1994.

Kegan, Robert, and Lisa Lahey. *How the Way We Talk Can Change the Way We Work: The Seven Languages for Transformation*. San Francisco, CA: Jossey-Bass, 2001.

Kingsolver, Barbara. "Civil Disobedience at the Breakfast Table." *High Tide in Tucson*. New York NY: Harper Perennial, 1996.

Learning Theories. "Maslow's Hierarchy of Needs." July 18, 2014. https://www.learning-theories.com/maslows-hierarchy-of-needs.html.

Losse, Kate. "The Art of Failing Upward." *New York Times*, March 5, 2016. https://www.nytimes.com/2016/03/06/opinion/sunday/the-art-of-failing-upward.html.

Meltzer, Lynn, ed. "Teaching Metacognitive Strategies That Address Executive Function Processes." *Executive Function in Education: From Theory to Practice*. New York, NY: The Guilford Press, 2007.

Mogel, Wendy. *The Blessing of a B Minus: Using Jewish Teachings to Raise Self-Reliant Children*. New York, NY: Simon & Schuster, 2010.

Mogel, Wendy *The Blessing of a Skinned Knee*. New York, NY: Simon & Schuster, 2001.

National Council of Teachers of English. "Fifty Alternatives to the Book Report." January, 1998. http://www.ncte.org/library/NCTEFiles/Resources/Journals/EJ/0871-jan98/EJ0871Ideas.PDF.

National Institute of Mental Health. "Obsessive Compulsive Disorder." Last updated January, 2016. https://www.nimh.nih .gov/health/topics/obsessive-compulsive-disorder-ocd/index .shtml.

National Scientific Council on the Developing Child. "Building the 'Brain's Air Traffic Control' System: How Early Experiences Shape the Development of Executive Function." Working Paper 11, Working Paper Series, Center on the Developing Child, Harvard University, May, 2011. http://developingchild .harvard.edu/wp-content/uploads/2011/05/How-Early-Experiences-Shape-the-Development-of-Executive-Function.pdf.

Park, Denise C., and Gérard N. Bischof. "The Aging Mind: Neuroplasticity in Response to Cognitive Training." *Dialogues in Clinical Neuroscience* 15, no. 1 (March, 2013). https://www.ncbi .nlm.nih.gov/pmc/articles/PMC3622463/.

Paulus, Trina. *Hope for the Flowers.* Manwah, NJ: Paulist Press, 1973.

Potok, Chaim. *In the Beginning.* New York, NY: Fawcett Books, 1975.

Prochaska, James O., Norcross, John C., and DiClemente, Carlo C. *Changing for Good: A Revolutionary Six-Stage Program for Overcoming Bad Habits and Moving Your Life Positively Forward.* New York, NY: First Avon Books, 1995.

Prochaska, James O., and Janice M. Prochaska. *Changing to Thrive: Using the Stages of Change to Overcome the Top Threats to Your Health and Happiness.* Center City, MN: Hazelden Publishing, 2016.

Rimer, Sara. "The Biology of Emotion—and What it May Teach Us about Helping People to Live Longer." *Harvard Public Health* magazine, Winter, 2011. https://www.hsph.harvard.edu/news/ magazine/happiness-stress-heart-disease/.

Sapolsky, Robert. *Why Zebras Don't Get Ulcers: The Acclaimed Guide to Stress, Stress-Related Diseases and Coping.* New York, NY: Holt Paperbacks, 1994.

Seiter, Courtney. "24 Free Apps To Help You Change Your Habits." *Fast Company,* January 14, 2015. https://www.fastcompany.com/ 3040819/24-free-apps-to-help-you-change-your-habits.

Siegel, Daniel, and Tina Payne-Bryson. *The Whole-Brain Child: 12 Revolutionary Strategies to Nurture Your Child's Developing Mind.* New York, NY: Bantam Books, 2012.

Steinberg, Laurence. *Age of Opportunity: Lessons from the New Science of Adolescence.* New York, NY: Houghton Mifflin Harcourt, 2014.

Wallace, Kelly. "Teens Spend a 'Mind-Boggling' 9 Hours a Day Using Media, Report Says." *CNN,* November 3, 2015, 9:07 p.m. EST. http://www.cnn.com/2015/11/03/health/teens-tweens-media-screen-use-report/index.html.

Zimmerman, B. J. "Models of Self-Regulated Learning and Academic Achievement." In *Self Regulated Learning and Academic Achievement,* edited by B. J. Zimmerman and D. H. Schunk. New York, NY: Springer, 1989.